From Surviving to Thriving in a Romantic Relationship

How to Reignite the Passion and keep the Magic Alive even when the Journey gets Tough

Wendy Capewell

The Relationship Specialist

From Surviving to Thriving in a Romantic Relationship
How to Reignite the Passion and keep the Magic Alive even when the Journey gets Tough

First published in 2016
Wendy Capewell, The Relationship Specialist
Copyright © Wendy Capewell 2016

The rights of the author has been asserted in accordance with Sections 77 and 78 of the Copyright Designs and Patents Act, 1988.

All rights reserved.
No part of this book may be reproduced (including photocopying or storing in any medium by electronic means and whether or not transiently or incidentally to some other use of this publication) without the written permission of the copyright holder except in accordance with the provisions of the Copyright, design and Patents Act 1988. Applications for the Copyright holder's written permission to reproduce any part of this publication should be addresses to the publishers.

ISBN-13: 978-1540467003

WHY YOU SHOULD READ THIS BOOK

This book is perfect for you if you want to understand the reasons why your relationships falter at times. It looks at why you continue to follow the same unhelpful pathways.

Based on my own personal life experiences, and my many years of working with clients on a professional basis, I have put together my insights of those issues that cause problems in relationships, and how to tackle them, so that you and your partner have a happier, closer and more loving relationship. I want to help you bring back the passion and magic that might have disappeared along the way.

When we first meet and fall in love with that special person, we truly believe that we are going to be happy. We believe we can surmount any problems that we may encounter. Unfortunately, that is rarely true. We often don't know what to do to resolve them.

This book will help you do just that.

I take you through the journey of a romantic relationship, exploring events on that journey that can cause stress in the relationship. There are also some case studies to help illustrate points. These are based on problems clients have brought to me, but are fictional case studies due to client confidentiality. I offer practical solutions to help you handle issues in a more helpful way. I've included some exercises in the book to help you.

Wendy

DEDICATION

To my beautiful daughters, friends, partners and clients. I want to thank each and every one of you for enriching my life, and adding to my experience, which has also allowed me to help and support those people who want to make changes and improve their relationships

FOREWORD

According to a report issued by the Office for National Statistics (ONS), the divorce rate in England and Wales increased during 2012 with approximately 13 divorces an hour being granted. The report said this was possibly because of the last recession, (2008/2009). Almost half of these divorces occurred in the first 10 years of marriage and increased stress was cited as a contributing factor. (*Divorce rate up 'because of recession', report says, BBC NEWS 6th February, 2014*)

I would say that this is, in part, down to the fast paced world in which we live, the rapid advancement of technology and a distinct lack of communication as originally intended. By that I mean the art of communication - actually speaking and listening to one another.

How many friends or family members do you know who get up in the morning, and go flying out of the door on their way to work without a word – just a series of grunts?? Perhaps even looking down at a screen on a mobile device that seems to have become a permanently linked appendage? Often communicating by text or even email that can be misconstrued because they are quite simply flat, devoid of tone and emotion.

Communication is a major factor in, any and all relationships, especially those where two people are joined by marriage or some other commitment. A breakdown in communication is an overwhelming stress factor. Stress is cited as significant in breakdowns connected with relationships and health.

You may wonder who am I to say this? Briefly, I too work with people who have relationship issues. As an Energy Psychologist, I specialise as a Mindset Coach and Wellness Practitioner. I believe in the power of the mind. Our mind is our most powerful asset; everything we do begins with a single thought. When we transmute that thought into action, 'things' begin to happen. Throw 'feeling and believing' into the mix and all sorts of things are possible! It's how records are broken, inventions come to fruition, and goals, whatever they may be, are achieved!

Fortunately, Wendy, and others like her can be a blessing. With the background of an experienced counsellor and psychotherapist, Wendy draws not only on her professional skills, but also her own life experiences, some of which she shares quite openly in this book. Indeed, it is her life experience, her training and her work that has channelled her into specialising in working with couples who are facing difficulties in their relationship that has compelled her to write this book.

Wendy takes you on a journey, through a series of possible events that as a couple you may encounter, that have the potential to cause conflict and unless resolved, can contribute to the breakdown of the relationship.

She also guides you through the numerous possibilities that exist to recover from a relationship breakdown, yet offers no illusions or guarantees that every couple she works with reconciles their differences and lives happily ever after. Sometimes separation and ultimately divorce is the only answer. Wendy touches briefly on surviving on your own should this happen.

Throughout the book, Wendy provides hints and tips and exercises to enable a once happy, healthy relationship to bounce back again. She asks challenging questions too, to get you thinking about the part you played in the relationship breakdown, it is never down to just one person. It takes two to tango. It takes two to make or break a relationship.

Given the right help and guidance and a willingness of both parties to take responsibility to re-ignite their relationship, it can and does happen. Wendy Capewell is perfectly placed to help people do just that.

This is a great book for those who wish to either avoid

a relationship breakdown, or who are seeking to repair one. Equally, it is a great book for parents to introduce their teenage children to, as they embark on their first intimate relationship, or even into marriage; especially if the parents have, or have had, relationship difficulties, as it is a way of highlighting potential relationship pitfalls and how to cope with them, that they may not be able to put into words that their child or children will either understand or accept. It is also a great book to pass on to a family member or friend who is experiencing relationship difficulties.

It is not, nor do I believe it is intended to be, a substitute to working with someone who is experienced and professionally qualified to help with relationship difficulties. Someone like Wendy.

I would just like to end by saying thank you to Wendy, for inviting me and trusting in me to write this foreword. It says a lot about our relationship.

To you the reader, you are more than likely reading this book because you have decided to take action, and I applaud you for that.

May you, the reader, take what you need from this book, as you seek the guidance you require in resolving your relationship difficulties. Whether you choose to resolve your difficulties together or separately, may you do so in such a way, that provides the best outcome for each of you, to Live YOUR best life!

Drew Ryder
Mindset Coach and Wellness Practitioner
www.drewryder.com

HOW TO USE THIS BOOK

My aim in this book is to take you through my view of the journey of a relationship. I know that each person who reads it will be on a different part of that journey. So instead of reading it from cover to cover, you may find it more useful to dip in and out of it and select the parts that are the most helpful for you. It doesn't matter whether you agree with what I have to say – what is far more relevant is that it gets you thinking about your relationship, and the way you interact within it. I want you to think about whether there is another way of being, or if the actions you are taking are the most helpful ones.

I have suggested some exercises along the way that you can try and there is a Resources section at the end for further help and support.

"I need to understand myself, and that this relationship is the foremost, most important one. Because, until I understand and learn to love myself, warts and all, I cannot possibly have a healthy, loving relationship with anyone else."

CONTENTS

Introduction

1	So, What's The Attraction?	Pg 1
2	All Consuming Romantic Love	Pg 3
3	The Bubble Bursts And Reality Kicks In	Pg 5
4	The Baggage We Carry Into Our Relationships	Pg 9
5	When Arguments And Disagreements Make Life Miserable	Pg 14
6	The 3 C's Vital In A Healthy Relationship	Pg 19
7	Relationships Need Attention And Nurturing	Pg 24
8	The Relationship Deepens	Pg 28
9	Moving In Together	Pg 29
10	Planning A Wedding	Pg 38
11	A New Arrival Can Be A Blessing As Well As A Curse	Pg 44
12	Blended Families	Pg 48
13	I Need Time On My Own!	Pg 51
14	The Power Struggle	Pg 54
15	Good News – There Is Another Way!	Pg 59
16	Is This Really Ok In A Relationship?	Pg 64
17	Affairs Can Be Complex	Pg 69

From Surviving to Thriving in a Romantic Relationship

18	Moving Forward And Building A Great Relationship	Pg 75
19	Bringing Back The Passion And Intimacy In The Bedroom	Pg 79
20	The Greatest Block – Vulnerability!	Pg 83
21	Passion Brings Great Sex	Pg 85
22	The Only Way Is Out	Pg 89
23	Surviving On Your Own	Pg 91
	Conclusion	Pg 96
	Connect With Me	Pg 97
	Acknowledgements	Pg 98
	About The Author	Pg 100
	Testimonials	Pg 101
	Resources & Further Reading	Pg 103

INTRODUCTION

Writing this book has been quite an emotional journey as it has been compiled from my own personal life experiences, together with those of my clients.

And of course I have studied and researched a great deal.

When I married at the age of 22, I had a very romantic view of marriage. The fantasy was all planned in my head. An idyllic life together, with our children, living in a house in the country, living happily ever after. That was **my** dream – **my** fantasy. Despite having been brought up by parents who had an unhappy marriage, no way was this going to happen to me.

At the beginning, it was like that. Life was fun, despite having hardly any money. We experienced the usual struggles that young couples encounter when first living together. There was a period of adjustment, which caused a few arguments, but nothing serious. We had two beautiful daughters, and moved to my dream house in the heart of a village in Surrey. Life was good.

As a result, when my husband told me he wanted to leave me after 10 years, it was a complete shock. I really didn't know how to handle it or where to turn for help. Sadly, despite trying to work it out between us, the marriage ended in divorce 4 years later.

Fast forward several years, and I married again, feeling I was older and wiser, and better equipped. How wrong I was! It seemed I hadn't learned very much at all about myself or relationships. It was an abusive relationship that ended in a very messy divorce.

These destructive patterns needed to stop. I wanted to

learn about me, and how I had played a part in the breakdown of those relationships.

So began my journey of self-discovery. Little did I realise, at that point, the path this would lead me to.

The first thing I learned is that the most important relationship is with ourselves. If I don't learn about how I function in the world, and learn to accept and love myself for who I am, then how can I begin to accept or love someone else?

After four years of training, I qualified as a counsellor and psychotherapist. Initially, I worked with individuals, and it soon became apparent that many of my clients' issues included relationship problems. Couples were also approaching me for help. It was time to seek out more specialised training.

I have spent several years studying, researching and learning more about what makes some relationships more successful than others. I discovered how our early family systems can have a profound effect on us, and that the experiences in previous relationships can influence our current ones, often recreating those same negative patterns we learned from them.

I explored what attracts us to each other, what binds us together, and makes for those strong bonds that serve us well when the going gets tough. I then began working with couples, as well as individuals, to help them work through the issues that they struggled with, helping them find the blocks that get in the way of sustaining a healthy relationship. I encourage them to move forward in a healthier, happier life, either together and at times apart – where that is the best solution for each of them.

Helping people form and sustain healthy relationships has been and continues to be my passion, and I love it!

Having personally been through many of the issues clients bring to me, I feel I am able to identify and connect with them. Saying that, I recognise that we are all unique, and each couples' experiences will be as different as each of them. So it's important that I take the time to understand their struggles and work with them to identify the triggers. We uncover the deep rooted problems that are the cause, rather than just addressing the symptoms. Together we develop ways in which they can overcome their difficulties in a way that works for them, and fits with their unique relationship.

So why write this book?

We don't get a manual when we start a relationship, and to be honest, we probably feel we don't need one. We believe everything will be great, because we are so madly in love. But my experience – both personal and professional – is that things don't always go the way we think they will. This can cause all kinds of problems that we find difficult to deal with.

My main focus is working one to one on a personal basis, helping people work through their relationship situations, which is very effective, especially as I can hone in on their specific problems and help find the best solutions for them.

However, for some people this can feel very intrusive and embarrassing. So this book is about some of the emotional and practical issues encountered on the journey of a romantic relationship, with some suggestions on how you might overcome them. I also quote some case studies, which are based on examples clients may bring, and so are not real cases. It's a guide and self-help book with some exercises you may find useful.

SO, WHAT'S THE ATTRACTION?

"Love recognizes no barriers. It jumps hurdles, leaps fences, penetrates walls to arrive at its destination full of hope." – Maya Angelou

When we first meet someone, there is often a physical attraction. Perhaps the other person has lovely eyes or smile, or we are drawn by their physique. We may also be attracted by the way we laugh at the same jokes, enjoy the same activities, have the same interests, appearing to agree on everything. In fact, it seems we have met the person of our dreams – the one we have been searching for.

What you may not be aware of is that we are also drawn to people by their smell. This is the work of pheromones, chemicals we produce. They are airborne, and transmitted to others of the same species in this way. For example, in mammals it's the way in which males and females make it known they are ready to mate.

These signals do not appear as strongly in humans, but they are ever present, even though we try to cover the natural odours by showering them away and masking them with perfumes, suppressing them with deodorants. Despite this, the odours that attract us to each other still get through.

So you can see some of the attraction we feel for others is out of our control, and would explain why we are drawn so strongly to one person rather than another.

WENDY CAPEWELL

*"You feel you have found the person of your dreams –
it must be destiny"*

ALL CONSUMING ROMANTIC LOVE

We may initially feel an instant attraction towards each other, or perhaps it's more of a slow burn. But when those overwhelming feelings of love and passion arise we become completely consumed by each other. This new love occupies every part of our waking day. We cannot sleep, eat or concentrate on much anything else.

I love the following quote. It sums up romantic love for me.

> *"There is never a time or place for true love. It happens accidentally, in a heartbeat, in a single flashing, throbbing moment." - Sarah Dessen, American Novelist*

Think about what it is that attracts you to another person, maybe in the past or your current partner.

LIST BELOW THOSE THINGS THAT ATTRACTED YOU TO YOUR PARTNER

_____

_____

_____

_____

At the beginning, love seems effortless and easy. Enjoying each other's company, wanting to be with each other all the time. It's delicious, exciting, passionate, absorbing, heart-stopping, and much, much more. You never felt you could be this happy.

You feel you agree on almost everything and you don't notice any little niggles that arise. In fact, they seem quirky and endearing, and almost add to the other's attraction. At other times, they don't seem important. You forgive any minor irritations, hardly noticing them, and at other times dismissing them.

Sex is great, if not awesome and you feel consumed by passion and romance. You feel engulfed by the closeness and intimacy you are sharing. It's interesting to notice that at this point in the new relationship, sex is often more about getting your needs met – your carnal satisfaction – rather than giving pleasure to your partner.

Passion is enhanced by the fact that you are still unsure about each other. It's rather like a dance – like a passionate Argentinian Tango – a dance of tension, each experiencing captivating intimacy and desire, at the same time unsure how long the dance will continue, and whether you can continue to stay in step.

As the relationship deepens, you begin to fantasise about a future together. You may playfully bring subjects up, throwing nuances and comments into conversation, testing the water. Some of the safer ones being about planning holidays together, the riskier comments may be about living together, marriage, a family.

You start visualising what it might be like to spend the rest of your lives together. For surely, that is the next step.

It all seems idyllic; you are totally in step with each other. Your friends and family make comments about how good you are together, saying you are made for each other. They maybe envious of you as you don't argue like they do.

THE BUBBLE BURSTS AND REALITY KICKS IN

As magical, delicious and wonderful as this romantic stage is, it can't and doesn't last. At this point I may have burst your bubble, and I'm sure that part of you is feeling I am mistaken, that you won't allow this to happen in your relationship; yours is different. You feel so totally happy that it can't happen to you.

The truth of the matter is that no relationship can sustain that level of all-consuming love and desire. As the reality kicks in, and we settle into daily life, we will have differences of opinion, and there will be conflict at times. We each realise that the other isn't perfect, and that relationships change with time.

I want to reassure you that this doesn't have to mean the end of romance and passion, or the relationship. It does mean you will need to put some work into the relationship, which thus far has been quite effortless and easy. And the good news is that it has the ability to develop into a richer, more fulfilling partnership, that is far more intimate than you have experienced. A long-lasting deeper love, where you each learn more about each other, continually.

In the following chapters we will explore the issues and difficulties that can arise, and ways in which you can deal with them in positive ways.

The Beginning of the Real Relationship

This is where the journey of a real committed relationship begins, where you start to build a deeper life together. It will certainly be full of bumps and potholes, as well as the high spots – times when you wish you could stop longer and enjoy the moment. There will be mountains to climb, which at times will seem insurmountable. Times when things get so bad you will wonder why you are in this relationship, and even with this person!

At these times, it's important that you have laid the foundations, and that your core beliefs are in line with each other.

If the foundations of your relationship are built on weak and unsustainable foundations, the journey will be much harder, and even unachievable.

What Makes You and Your Partner Tick?

Do you really know what your values and core beliefs are, what makes you the person you are?.

WHAT ARE YOUR CORE BELIEFS AND VALUES?

SELECT FROM THE LIST BELOW AND ADD ANY OTHERS THAT ARE IMPORTANT TO YOU, PUTTING THEM IN ORDER OF IMPORTANCE

Adventure	Integrity	_____
Affection	Justice	_____
Bigotry	Leadership	_____
Calm	Leisure Pursuits	_____
Confidence	Love	_____
Culture	Loyalty	_____
Education	Masculinity/ Femininity	_____
Environment	Nature	_____
Equality	Privacy	_____
Fidelity	Qualifications	_____
Financial Security	Professional Development	_____
Friendships	Religion	_____
Happiness	Responsibility	_____
Health	Safety	_____
Honesty	Self-Esteem	_____
Human Rights	Sensitivity	_____
Independence	Status	_____
Inner Peace	Other	_____

Only when you really know these will you begin to know which ones fit – and which don't – with your partner, or a future partner. Because it's those that will help sustain a relationship through the bad times.

I am not necessarily talking about hobbies or interests as they can change over time. It's much deeper than that.

For me, they include trust, integrity, honesty, our beautiful planet and the way we treat it. I abhor bigotry in any shape or form, and will fight for justice, equality and human rights. My family is very precious to me, as are my friends. I am not particularly materialistic, preferring to experience life, rather than things.

As for my personality, I am sensitive and emotional, passionate and tenacious, and I recognise these traits can work in my favour as well as against me at times.

Once you understand yourself and your core values, start to think about what kind of core values a potential partner has. If they are completely at odds with yours, you may want to consider whether this partnership is the right one for you. Will they affect your relationship to such a degree they will cause continual upsets? Do you have the ability to cope with them?

> **LIST THE CORE BELIEFS AND VALUES YOU CONSIDER IMPORTANT IN A PARTNER**
>
> _____
> _____
> _____
> _____
> _____
> _____

THE BAGGAGE WE CARRY INTO OUR RELATIONSHIPS

When I hear people say they don't have any baggage, I inwardly chuckle to myself, because each of our lives are coloured by our family systems and early life experiences. As a result, they affect the way in which we function as adults.

There is a very famous British psychologist, psychiatrist, and psychoanalyst, called John Bowlby, who is known for his interest in child development. His Attachment Theory suggests that the type of emotional attachment formed in childhood with their caregiver affects the way adults form attachments in their relationships.

The ideal style of attachment is a secure attachment, where your caregiver is emotionally and physically available for the child and that they are in tune with their child's emotions. Their child can count on the caregiver to be supportive and loving, at the same time allowing the child to grow and develop, and become independent, with strong boundaries.

Few of us have experienced a Secure Attachment style from our caregiver, and they would probably not be aware of any of this.

Below are listed the different styles you may have experienced, although they can be a mixture.

For example, my mother's style of attachment was a mixture of Avoidant and Ambivalent.

Secure
- Aligned with the child; in tune with the child's emotions
- Able to create meaningful relationships; empathetic; able to set appropriate boundaries

Avoidant
- Unavailable or rejecting
- Avoids closeness or emotional connection; distant; critical; rigid; intolerant

Ambivalent
- Inconsistent and sometimes intrusive parent communication
- Anxious and insecure; controlling; blaming; erratic; unpredictable; sometimes charming

Disorganized
- Ignored or didn't see child's needs was frightening/traumatizing parental behaviour
- Chaotic; insensitive; explosive; abusive; untrusting even while craving security

Reactive
- Extremely unattached or malfunctioning
- Cannot establish positive relationships

Emma's Story

Emma's childhood experiences impacted a lot on her adult relationships and the choices she made.

She was attracted to 'bad boys' whom she saw as being exciting and fun. However, they treated her badly, one cheating on her with other women, whilst promising never to do it again. Emma became very anxious and distrustful of her partner, checking up on him all the time. This caused continual arguments. In the end, her partner left her for another woman.

In another relationship, Emma found herself continually starting arguments over trivial things. She would pick a fight for no apparent reason. Unconsciously, she was testing him to see if he really would stay around. In the end, she succeeded in getting the result she really didn't want, but expected. Her partner walked out.

Emma's behaviour in her relationships was a result of her childhood experiences. Her lack of trust of her partner was based on her trust being broken by her father when he failed to keep to arrangements. She also made unhealthy choices in the men she had relationships with, as they were not likely to be the kind of men who would commit. She found it hard to commit to a relationship, at the same time craving the security she missed as a child.

Emma's mother's choices of male partners coloured Emma's choices. Witnessing men treating her mother badly left her believing all men treated women badly.

How different attachment styles can affect adult characteristics

Secure Attachment style:
- Able to create meaningful relationships, empathetic, able to set appropriate boundaries.

Avoidant Attachment style:
- Avoids closeness or emotional connection, distant, critical, rigid, intolerant.

Ambivalent Attachment style:
- Anxious and insecure, controlling, blaming, erratic, unpredictable, sometimes charming.

Disorganized Attachment style:
- Parental style: Ignored or didn't see child's needs, parental behaviour was frightening/traumatizing.
- Resulting adult characteristics: Chaotic, insensitive, explosive, abusive, untrusting even while craving security.

Reactive Attachment style:
- Cannot establish positive relationships, often misdiagnosed.

Adding to the Baggage

Our family system is the only one we make sense of, and for us it's normal, the way all families work.

If we were beaten and ill-treated as a child, our understanding is that it's what happens to all children. Sadly, this can colour the way we behave in adulthood, and the way we treat our children. Luckily this is not always true, as most adults recognise how damaging that behaviour is and want to do something better.

If mum did everything for the family, not expecting anyone to help with chores, or clean and tidy up after others, we are likely to believe that this is how all families operate. And so as an adult we will fall into the same patterns. A woman who does everything for her partner and a guy who assumes that this is how the world works, and allows it.

If our parents spent all their time together, never having other friends outside their relationship, then we are likely to see that as normal.

Experiencing parents who constantly argued, maybe heatedly, will be normal for us. Conversely, if parents never argued, just brushing issues under the carpet, that will be normal to us.

The thing is that problems can arise when we meet and join with someone else. Because their family system is likely to be different from ours, it can often create conflict and a Power Struggle, which I talk about indepth in

Chapter 14, can rear its ugly head. This happens without us even realising it.

At the beginning of a relationship, we are only too happy to do things for each other, wanting to please this special person with whom we have fallen madly in love. However, after a while, we may begin to feel that things don't fit with how we think things should be done. It doesn't fit with our experience of how a relationship should work.

We do things in a particular way, and expect our partner to respond in the way we know. When they don't, it can cause confusion and often arguments.

We need to understand how we behave in relationships, and where that behaviour came from, as well as talking things through with our partner and firstly understanding their perception of things and then working together to build our family system. Our way isn't always the only – or right – way. Working together, learning about each other, and accepting that our partner has their way of operating in the world, we are better equipped to build a strong, loving partnership. One in which there is mutual respect for each other.

Exploring our core values, and family systems can help us identify why we behave in a particular way, and how we fall into unhealthy relationships.

WHEN ARGUMENTS AND DISAGREEMENTS MAKE LIFE MISERABLE

Conflict can arise at any point during an intimate, deep partnership. Where there has been smooth sailing during the initial stages of a relationship, and a sense of harmony, a big change or event may well trigger arguments. As a result, it can cause stress when these things happen.

Common triggers –
- Getting married – the wedding
- A new baby
- Moving in together
- Redundancy
- A change in working situations – such as a partner being around more or less due to their job, which could involve working away, or being at home more often. Redundancy can have a profound effect not only on the individual but also on the relationship.
- Empty Nest Syndrome - when the children have left home
- One of you losing your job
- Moving house
- Illness
- Death in the family

At times when conflict arises, we may question ourselves, wondering whether it's us that is at fault. Maybe we are concerned that we are too picky, wanting things all our own way. Feeling that we need to be more understanding. In some cases, that could be true. So it's worth checking it out and being honest with ourselves.

However, also be mindful if your partner puts all the blame onto you, rather than taking responsibility for their part.

It's at times like this that we begin to remember how wonderful it was at the start of the relationship. We start comparing those times with the present ones, and start searching for the connection we had together then. We try to reconstruct it. However hard we try, it just doesn't seem to happen. The passion and romance we experienced then seems to have dwindled.

Feelings of unhappiness begin to creep in. Feelings of being robbed of something very precious rise to the surface, craving the intimacy and closeness that no longer seems to be there.

During these times we can feel scared that we have shown our vulnerability to someone we don't even recognise anymore. So, we begin to withdraw – from them and the relationship – feeling confused. We start to wonder whether we want to stay or leave. It can feel really uncomfortable. We may feel scared of the intimacy we once shared, and so the physical side of the relationship may suffer, passion dwindling. At the same time, we have a desire to be close again.

So much confusion!

My Experience

"I recall that craving of wanting back the person I first met and fell madly in love with. I felt rejected, wondering why it felt like he didn't want to be with me, what was wrong with me. And of course I took it all upon myself. I had to be to blame as that was the place I recognised from childhood – not being good enough."

And it is something I hear many times from clients I work with. The reality is, when we first met, we were projecting onto each other our unrealistic desires and fantasies. The reality is that neither of us can live up to that.

It's no wonder that we withdraw from each other, not wanting to feel hurt, and scared of being intimate as we feel very vulnerable, having opened up and bared our soul to each other.

Because of those feelings of rejection and confusion, disagreements start arising. We start to question what we are doing in the relationship and with this person. Minor niggles turn into bigger rows, as each person defends their corner, not wanting to back down. Because by doing so, we may lose our identity and sense of self altogether. Our confidence is affected and we begin to doubt our ability to make sensible decisions. How could we have picked the wrong person? How did we get it so wrong?

We start to feel resentment towards our partner, angry or frustrated about all we have done for them, or given up for what we perceived as the person of our dreams. We begin to feel taken for granted – a door mat. This can turn into accusations as our hurt and disappointment bubbles up.

Not only do we withdraw, but we may even feel hostile towards each other. At these times it's important that we have a strong enough bond to be able to navigate through the tough times. Being able to talk to each other openly and honestly is the best way forward, which I explore more in Chapter 13.

MY **E**XPERIENCE

"I really felt I was the problem! I clearly recall feeling it was because I was an unlovable child. My father didn't spend any time with me, he never cuddled or hugged me, never had conversations with me, or made me feel special.

"What I didn't realise at the time was he was suffering from PTSD. Yes, I understood he had fought in the 2nd World War, seen and experienced some horrendous things. He had been captured twice and imprisoned in prisoner of war camps. Because of those awful experiences, he had disconnected emotionally. But as a child, I had no comprehension of the brevity of it all. I just felt I was unlovable. This feeling followed me into adulthood, until I realised it wasn't about me; these were my dad's issues, which sadly he struggled with for the rest of his life, including a mental breakdown."

We have to accept our parents did the best they could with the tools they had available to them.

Don't drag others into your dramas

When feeling unhappy in our relationships, it's tempting to turn to others, like friends and family, to get them on side, hoping to get reassurance and validation for our feelings.

A word of warning here – before doing so, check out your motivation for talking to someone, because it can cause more problems than it resolves.

Are you looking for someone to agree with you that you are the wounded person, and that your partner is being unreasonable? Or do you want to brainstorm your feelings, and are able to come to your own conclusions once you have ordered your thoughts? Also remember that if you do talk to others about your concerns, and then later resolve the problems, it can cause rifts between your partner and your family and friends.

What works in your relationship may not work for others. So, be cautious about your motives, and choose carefully those you share your problems with. Make sure it's someone who is likely to have a balanced perspective of things, rather than offering an emotional response.

The best way to resolve issues is to talk with your partner about the problems, after all, it's your relationship, and you are the only ones who can find a solution that works satisfactorily for your relationship

THE 3 C's VITAL IN A HEALTHY RELATIONSHIP

I believe there are three basic ingredients needed in a committed relationship for it to be healthy and successful.

1. Commitment
2. Caring
3. Communication

If any of these are lacking, then don't ignore the situation, work on that area. If all three are missing, then the relationship is in real trouble, and you may have to really consider whether this relationship is ever going to work, unless both of you are prepared to make some huge changes.

1. Commitment

Are you really committed to the relationship? This means more than fidelity and exclusion of all others in a romantic and intimate way. Being committed is about being willing to put in the effort and intention to make this relationship work. It's about you and your partner being truly invested in it, working as a team, through the tough times as well as the happy times. Trusting each other to be honest and faithful, and feeling safe enough to put your trust in your partner.

2. Caring

Ask yourself if you love each other, but also whether you are in love with each other. Do you demonstrate care and love for your partner on a daily basis? Of course words are important, but behaviour and gestures speak volumes. Acts of kindness, affection, generosity, loyalty, self-sacrifice, understanding and empathy, support and encouragement all demonstrate your care and love for each other.

Intimacy and sex are important in a romantic relationship too, but you cannot build a relationship on sex alone. That kind of relationship will be far too shallow, as well as unsustainable. Read more about sex and intimacy in Chapter 17.

Friendship is a major factor in any relationship. It doesn't mean you have to be joined at the hip, sharing every single leisure or hobby. That would lead to the relationship feeling claustrophobic. However, it does mean experiencing enjoyment in each other's company, as well as there being elements of mutual support and fun.

I love allowing my Inner Child out to play. There is nothing more enjoyable than just having uninhibited fun. Whether with a partner, friend, or child, let's face it laughter is one of the best medicines.

3. Communication

This is much deeper than talking on a superficial level about the daily issues in life. Communication is being able to talk to each other about your deeper thoughts, dreams and aspirations, without being judged or put down. Talking to each other about the things that aren't going so well, and working together to find ways to resolve them is key.

It's also being interested in what each other thinks and feels, and not being dismissive if you don't 'get' how each other feels, or don't agree with their beliefs. By being able to listen to each other's concerns within the relationship, without being dismissive and trying to understand each other's feelings, you will build a strong and more intimate bond.

Having respect and regard for each other as individuals in their own right allows each of you to grow.

How often do you hear someone saying of their partner, 'I know what you are thinking!'

However well you know each other, you can't possibly know what someone is thinking or is going to say, and it's disrespectful to each other to say that. There is nothing more galling than someone telling you this.

So, allow your partner to speak for themselves, instead of assuming you know what they are thinking or are going to say. Listen carefully, you may be surprised and hear something you had previously not heard.

ARE THE 3 C's PRESENT IN YOUR RELATIONSHIP?

In the boxes below, write down how each of the three Cs are present in your relationship.

COMMUNICATION

- How many times a week do you sit down and talk to your partner about your relationship – rather than about the daily issues in life?

- Do you talk to your partner about what is troubling you about your relationship?

- How often do you spend quality time with your partner, going out together on your own?

- Do you talk to your partner on a regular basis about personal, meaningful issues?

- How often do you talk to your partner rather than watch TV/text friends/play online games alone/bring work home?

CARING

- Do you make time for your partner when they phone you?

- How often do you initiate positive, loving physical contact with your partner?

- Do you greet your partner lovingly when you first meet?

- How often do you do something for your partner so they feel you really care about them?

- Are you available to your partner when they have a problem, to just be there and listen?

COMMITMENT

- Are you faithful to your partner to the exclusion of all others in a romantic, intimate and sexual way?

- Are you totally committed to putting in the effort to making your relationship work, even through the tough times?

- Do you demonstrate your honesty and trustworthiness?

- Do you work together as a team?

RELATIONSHIPS NEED ATTENTION AND NURTURING

Just as a small seedling requires a lot of loving care and attention – good soil, nutrients, water and light to grow into a healthy strong plant – a relationship also requires loving care and attention to grow into a strong solid partnership. As you would not neglect a seedling, forget to water it, or shove it in a dark cupboard, ignoring it and expecting it to flourish, neither would you expect a relationship to thrive if it wasn't given care and attention. That relationship will wither and die in time.

Life is busy and other things get in the way

Of course it isn't easy when we have such busy lives, pressurised jobs, caring for children as well as many other commitments we may have, such as taking care of aging parents. However, by putting our relationship on hold until the career gets off the ground, or the children are older and don't need so much attention, we may discover the relationship is no longer there.

How sad to discover you no longer have anything in common, you have grown apart and you are no longer able to communicate with each other. By becoming so engrossed in your own world, whether it be career, children, hobbies and outside interests, your relationship can easily become neglected. It can be a hard balancing act, juggling all the different areas of your life. The danger comes when you neglect your relationship, believing your partner will understand. Wrong! You need to pay attention, because your partner may not understand, and get fed up and leave. Hard work it may be, but it's well worth the investment.

So don't dismiss your partner when they complain you don't spend time with each other anymore. Don't put it down to jealousy, or selfishness on their part. Listen! And then have a discussion about it. Consider whether your partner has a valid point.

If you justify your feelings, are you really saying that your relationship is second best to everything else in your life?

Remember those wonderful crazy feelings you had when you first met?

Think about when you had a really good relationship, before things started to become mundane, or boring.

How did you treat each other? Now think about the way you behave towards each other now, and the way you talk to each other. Ask yourself whether you are respectful towards each other. I hear couples that don't talk 'to' each other, instead they talk 'at' each other. Have you got into bad habits of being disrespectful? You may have had a bad day but it doesn't mean you have to take it out on them! Once those harsh words are spoken, they cannot be taken back and they can really sting – often causing deep resentments that are hard to get over, leaving emotional scars.

- Speak to each other respectfully, and politely. Ask yourself if you would speak to a friend in the way you speak to your partner.
- Think about what you can do to make them feel loved and valued.
- Spend time together doing things you both enjoy, and even try new things.

Going out and spending time together as a family is

important, and it's nice to spend time with extended family and friends too. But it's equally important to spend time alone, just the two of you. After all it's your relationship, and the reason you got together in the first place. It's good just being together and sometimes just doing nothing together. So turn off the TV, ditch the laptop, tablet and phone for a few hours and reconnect with each other.

Saving up your time together for when you are on holiday, or a long weekend away, whilst quite nice, really isn't enough. Relationships need to be worked at continually. If I go back to the analogy of the seedling, you wouldn't expect it to survive on an annual watering.

Inject some romance into your relationship

Rather than just the mundane chatter that often happens, such as *'What do you want for dinner?'* or *'Have you put the bin out?'* Talk about meaningful subjects. Because if the level of conversing with each other is only about trivia, it will be hardly surprising if your relationship becomes boring. And it's likely that your sex life suffers too, as there is nothing less passionate than talking about cleaning toilets and grocery shopping.

WHAT CAN YOU DO TO REIGNITE YOUR RELATIONSHIP AND SHOW YOUR PARTNER YOU CARE?

HERE ARE SOME SUGGESTIONS BELOW TO START YOU THINKING

- A candlelit dinner at home
- A bath together
- Cuddles on the sofa
- Having meaningful conversations with each other
- Giving each other a massage
- Exploring new things together, whether hobbies, places, interests or sex.

THE RELATIONSHIP DEEPENS

As the relationship deepens, you may decide at some point that you want to make more of a commitment to each other. This can take many forms, including moving in together, getting engaged or marriage.

Each of these bring their challenges. At the outset, you probably don't see them as such, as you get caught up with the excitement of it all. You don't envisage there being problems and feel optimistic that you will get through anything, whatever it is, together.

So in the next few chapters I talk about some of the different events and what difficulties they can bring. Hopefully, by thinking about them and talking through possible problems that could arise beforehand, the issues may not be so problematic.

Each couple's journey will look different, and events are likely to be in a different order, or may not apply to you at all. Equally, there may be things I haven't covered.

MOVING IN TOGETHER

Exciting times! You feel the time is right to move in together. It could be that you move in with your partner into their existing home, or each other's family, or you find somewhere new to live together.

If one person moves into the other's existing home, it can raise some problems. The existing homeowner may unconsciously see their home as their 'territory', and their partner who is moving in as an interloper. So if your partner is moving in with you, be mindful of the fact that you will be established in your home, having your possessions in place, just where you like them. Your partner may feel wrong-footed, at a disadvantage as they will be the newcomer. They will want to bring their belongings into your home, which will now become your joint home, and they will want to feel accepted and not feel like a guest or worse – a stranger!

Have a conversation beforehand, talk about how you are going to handle the move. Make space for your partner, so they feel welcome. If space is an issue, be prepared to de-clutter and relinquish some of your possessions to make room for your partner's treasures.

If you are the one moving into your partner's home, have a discussion with them about the things you want to bring into the new home. Don't underestimate this. There is nothing worse than having resentments or arguments over belongings. Or, standing in the middle of the room wondering where on earth you are going to put everything. Be sensitive to each other. What may seem like complete tat to you, could be of real sentimental value to the other. And remember to negotiate!

> **HOW ARE YOU GOING TO HANDLE THE MOVE IN TOGETHER, WHAT THINGS DO YOU NEED TO THINK ABOUT AND DISCUSS?**
>
> _____
>
> _____
>
> _____
>
> _____
>
> _____

Sharing Chores

When couples move in together, they often believe that everything will fall magically into place. That all the boring stuff will take care of itself. Trust me, this rarely happens, and if it does, there will come a point when one or both of you are going to get fed up or resentful. Having been really happy to do everything for your partner at the start, you may begin to feel resentful, that you are doing more than your fair share.

You remember how I talked about family systems in Chapter 4, and the fact this is what you base your normal on? Because of this, you may fall into the trap of believing your new partner will fit in with your ways. This assumption is either based on the belief that all families operate in this way, or because you don't even consider there is another way – and anyway, you are used to operating in this manner and to change would be uncomfortable.

The problem here is that the new love in your life probably has their own way of being, which developed from their family system – and it's unlikely to be the same! The more easy-going person is probably going to be less bothered than one who likes things more orderly. This can include little things like washing up straight after the meal, to cleaning up after having a shower or bath. However trivial these things can be, especially said out loud, trust me, couples fall out about them.

When you are so absorbed in each other, talking about these subjects seems unimportant. After all, when there is so much passion flying around, issues about who cooks, washes up, cleans the toilet, does the shopping and maintains the garden don't really get talked about. And, they certainly don't go hand in hand with the romantic side of the relationship.

At first, you may willingly take on certain chores. After all you are madly in love with this person and you want to make them happy. You are probably still floating on the cloud of passion, and it all seems too trivial to discuss.

But if you don't tackle these things and negotiate who is doing what, resentments will set in. One person, if not both, will begin to feel they are doing the major share of the chores. Or that they are taking on all the responsibilities, whilst the other is sitting back allowing this to happen. Times of stress and tiredness can be trigger points for these kinds of arguments. We all get a little tetchy at such times. Our patience wears thin, and we become less reasonable.

Alternatively, it may not even register there is another way. Perhaps in the family you grew up in mum did all the cooking and dad looked after the finances? But it's an ever-changing world and this is a new relationship and time to create your own family system. You also need to remember that situations can change over time. Career changes, where there can be longer commuting time, illness, or having children can also change the dynamics in a relationship as well as the share of daily chores.

Yes, of course it's tiresome to have to sit down and talk about them, but if you don't, resentment grows, and arguments and bickering increase. One partner may feel they are being nagged at, and as a result switch off. The other could feel their complaints are falling on deaf ears.

It's so much better to address it. Negotiate with each other which chores each of you do, and feel comfortable doing. See it as teamwork rather than a competition. Don't forget to take into consideration your other responsibilities. It's important that each person doesn't feel they are doing it all, or more than they can cope with. That will lead to them feeling exhausted and put on, and the other let down. The plus side is that by working as a team, you will have more leisure time for yourself and together.

The other thing to be acutely aware of, is whether bickering over the trivial things is masking real issues you don't want to address. Is it easier to discuss who washes up rather than talking about your dissatisfaction with your sex life?

THINGS TO DISCUSS AROUND SHARING CHORES

_____

_____

_____

_____

_____

Sorting out the money

Money means different things to different people. Some people feel really anxious if they don't have a rainy day fund set aside, whilst others have an attitude that life is for living and they don't worry about money at all. They often spend to the limit on their credit cards and overdrafts.

I have worked with couples where financial issues have caused major problems in their relationship. The bottom line is often lack of understanding and consideration of each other's feelings or needs.

The responsibility for finances in a relationship may be taken on by one person. Perhaps because they have a financial background, or because they want that control. They could be worried the other has no money sense. That may suit the other person, as they don't have to take responsibility. That can work well whilst there is sufficient money to pay the bills at the end of each month.

However, when money problems arise, which can be due to a large unexpected bill, or some other financial crisis, the partner who hasn't been involved in dealing with the finances may not have a clue what the problem is – and possibly doesn't want to know. They just bury their head in the sand whilst the one who deals with money, juggles the money and gets more and more stressed. Credit cards max, as do overdrafts. This leads to arguments, together with constant money worries.

At other times, problems can arise when one person is earning less money than the other or not bringing financial contributions to the partnership. This can be because they are contributing by providing the childcare. Or because they are unable to find a job that brings in money. In some relationships there may be sufficient income that only one partner needs to work.

Take the situation where one person is earning less than the other. Does it seem fair that you each contribute equal amounts to the budget? Only you can decide that, as what suits one couple won't suit another. However, it is important that you have an open and honest discussion, and reach a manageable agreement where each of you are happy with the outcome.

If not addressed and things are left so they fester, it can lead to one of the following:

- Resentment and pressure from the one providing the major part of the family income
- A sense of inadequacy from the one having to ask for money to pay bills, leading to a sense of being the lesser person in the partnership, and lacking self-worth
- Continual bickering because one feels they are contributing more than the other, which can then lead to dishonesty and deceit, and hiding money from the other
- Where the 'earner' gives their partner an allowance each month, the partner receiving that allowance can suffer a real lack of self-worth. Perhaps feeling they are being treated like a child. The person providing the allowance may see themselves in a parental role, with their partner not taking responsibility.

So talk to each other and be honest about your feelings and negotiate between you how to manage the finances so you both feel comfortable and an equal partner.

> **WHAT ISSUES HAS THIS BROUGHT UP THAT YOU WANT TO TALK ABOUT TOGETHER?**
>
> _____
>
> _____
>
> _____
>
> _____
>
> _____
>
> _____

Planning a Budget

I certainly feel you need to decide a budget and work out all the outgoings for each month, as well as all income. Plan savings for a rainy day, holidays and emergencies too. To ignore this is very foolhardy and irresponsible, as debts can cause major problems, with repossession of goods and homes. Be honest with each other about any debts you have accumulated, or if you have been declared bankrupt, have any County Court Judgements, or bad credit rating. Not only will keeping it a secret cause upset, but it will also cause a lack of trust. By keeping a secret about one issue it can cause lack of trust in other areas of the relationship – eroding over time and becoming hard to repair.

You may decide to open a joint account into which each of you contribute an amount to pay bills. Together, you can decide which bills are to be paid out of this account, and which you will be responsible for alone.

Other couples prefer for each to share responsibility for outgoings, with each person paying some of the bills.

For example, one pays rent and groceries, and the other pays for utilities.

If one person takes sole responsibility for the financial side of the relationship, it can cause real problems if that person falls ill, or even worse, dies. Especially if the other cannot gain access to money. So even if one person does most of the managing, the other needs be included, and know the state of their finances, and be able to access funds in an emergency.

I have known couples who are not honest about money. One, having large sums stashed away that the other doesn't know about. This gives real cause for concern, and I wonder about the trust and commitment in the relationship.

When debt gets out of hand

I have witnessed many people who have run into debt, burying their heads in the sand, hoping it will go away on its own, or that they will be able to sort it out somehow. They have borrowed more and more money, even taking out payday loans. This leads to disaster. So if you find this happening to you, don't ignore it –seek advice. There is always free help and advice at the Citizens Advice Bureau, and they can often negotiate with creditors for a workable payment plan.

Below is the story that Bob and June brought to me.

Bob dealt with all the finances, making sure there were sufficient funds to pay the bills each month. June happily left him to it, and initially this worked. They had sufficient disposable income for it not to cause a problem. They were both working, and bringing in a good salary.

Then they decided to start a family and initially, June was on maternity leave, but then she had to make the decision to go back to work as they were just not managing. She took a part time job, but had to pay child care fees, and the baby needed things all the time. She also needed new work clothes. Bob said they couldn't afford all these things, so June put them on her credit card without telling Bob, so he was blissfully unaware June wasn't managing on their budget.

The crunch came when Bob found a letter from the credit card company. He was very angry, not only because June had run up a huge debt that now needed to be dealt with, but issues of trust arose. Arguments became very heated, almost leading to the complete breakdown of their relationship.

Fortunately, with help and support they were able to address the debt and trust issues, get the debt under control and work on the trust and secrecy issues.

In this situation, we worked together to address the issues around the mounting debt and secrecy. They got help to sort out their debt and the specialist advisor helped them with their budget, which eased the pressure on both of them.

They began talking to each other honestly, and once they did, they also began talking about the underlying issues that were causing problems in their relationship. Bob acknowledged that he didn't treat June as an equal. He admitted he was quite dictatorial, and he alone made decisions about most things in the relationship.

This led June to feel inferior and unable to talk to Bob when she couldn't manage on the money he allowed her. She felt too scared to talk to Bob about this, fearing he would explode – which he did in the end. Bob's childhood was from a family which was quite poor, and the bailiffs were often knocking on the door. Many times they removed items from the home, which made Bob scared. He was concerned that this could happen in his adult life and therefore strictly controlled the money.

Once they opened up to each other, they were able to understand where each other was coming from, and from then on they worked together on the finances.

PLANNING A WEDDING

What's involved

How exciting – you have decided to get married! You start planning the big day, and there is so much to think about.

- The date
- Venue – civil or religious ceremony
- Catering
- Guest list
- Choosing the major participants such as best man, bridesmaids
- Outfits
- Flowers
- The rings
- Photographs
- The cake…and the list goes on

As exciting as it can all be, it can also be extremely stressful. Weddings have become more and more elaborate – and costly – as couples vie to have the best, most expensive and more lavish event than their friends before them.

The tradition of the father of the bride paying for the wedding does not happen as often these days. This could be because parents have split up, or formed new relationships, and are supporting new families, as well as former ones, resulting in financial constraints all round, and certainly insufficient funds to pay for the wedding. Or maybe there is a change in financial circumstances, and parents are no longer in a situation to help financially – perhaps because of redundancy, or ill-health.

Wealthier families are often more able to foot the bill, whilst other families have saved over a period of years for their daughter's wedding. However, these days it seems far more usual for couples to pay for the wedding themselves.

Hen and stag parties

These too have become more extravagant, often turning into weekend events, with venues abroad. Lots of alcohol is often consumed and sadly there are times this evokes misunderstandings, arguments or even fights, which can then have repercussions for the wedding. Heated arguments preclude the great day with people falling out with each other and tensions arising. Where large amounts of alcohol are consumed during these events, it can lead to all kinds of problems. Alcohol lowers inhibitions, people's behaviour can become unreasonable. Men may get feisty and ready for a fight. At other times flirting or indiscretions occur. And if the bridegroom is involved in this it can lead to devastating consequences, and is certainly not a great start to married life. Whilst everyone who attends maybe sworn to secrecy, you can never be sure that someone will not spill the beans. So use alcohol wisely. Letting your hair down is one thing, but doing something you may regret and that has a negative impact on your relationship, or cancelling the wedding, is quite another.

Honeymoon

This too has become more and more lavish as couples decide to go further and further afield to exotic locations, adding to the mounting costs already incurred on the wedding.

"Spending vast amounts of money on a wedding does not mean it will make the marriage any better."

Huge debts incurred at the start of married life is not a great way to start.

Emotions, tantrums and dissatisfaction

Moving on to the emotional issues surrounding the great day, some of which I have experienced first-hand, as well as those by friends and family, including upsets and arguments about who should or should not be on the guest list.

Weddings really do evoke strong emotional feelings, and some interesting, if unpleasant, behaviours. Sometimes people feel snubbed when they are not invited, which can lead to others boycotting the wedding in protest. It all mars the event, making the lead up to what should be a joyful celebration, stressful and anxiety making. Unfortunately, people forget this is meant to be a happy celebration for the couple involved, and not a time for childlike tantrums. Disappointments happen – life is full of them.

There seems to be an increasing number of brides-to-be who feel they are not the right size or shape and so they launch themselves into a fitness and weight regime, adding to the building pressures already on them. I wonder why these women are not comfortable in their own skins, feeling they need to fit a media image of the 'perfect' bride. The person you marry loves you for the way you are, and if you want to look good for the wedding photos, just think about whether it will portray the real you.

I am curious about why couples crave such a fairy tale wedding, aiming for utopia. I wonder whether this is to falsely keep the magic alive – that Romantic Love they experienced at the start of their relationship?

Couples can get frustrated if and when things don't go to plan, (which is expecting a lot, for in real life mishaps happen and things go awry). Do the couple fear that if they don't have the fairy tale wedding it will break the spell? Are they reluctant to face the realities of life?

I also wonder if sometimes there is an element of peer pressure, of wanting to outdo others. Just who are they in competition with? I think the couple can lose sight of what a wedding is about, which can easily be fuelled by family and friends, their expectations and fantasies.

The Great Day arrives

The day arrives amid much excitement and angst. Will everyone involved be healthy and well for the day? Will either the bride or groom change their minds at the last minute? Heaven forbid!

I have heard of the wedding flowers being dead on arrival, the cake getting damaged on the way to the venue, the cars not turning up or breaking down, as well as many other mishaps. Unfortunately, this is called life; these things can and do happen. There is so much pressure on ensuring the day is perfect, it just adds to anxieties.

The most important thing to remember is that these things will only ruin your day if you choose to allow them to.

MY EXPERIENCE

I recall on the day of my wedding I went to the hairdresser's in the morning and then on to a friend's for a cuppa, mainly to avoid all the angst and mayhem occurring back at home, which I knew would be happening. It was a wise move as I returned to the house with everyone else in a tiz. I felt calm and relaxed and just disappeared into my bedroom to get ready, leaving the hubbub behind. I didn't want anything to upset me, and didn't allow it to. My mother was always stressed so it was good for me to keep my distance.

So for me it was a wonderful, magical day, one that I really enjoyed. I am sure it helped by starting my day in a calm and relaxed way.

It's a good idea to arrange beforehand some reliable friends who can deal with any problems if they arise, so that you can enjoy your day to its fullest. It's a very special day and one to be enjoyed.

RELIABLE FRIENDS YOU CAN DELEGATE TO

_____

_____

_____

_____

_____

_____

Make the most of the day whatever happens, and remember what it's really about. A day to make a commitment to your partner and celebrate your love for each other.

Two people joining together and making a commitment to stay together, loving and caring for each other, through the bad times as well as the good times. They invite their friends and family to witness and celebrate this.

The wedding night

After such an eventful day, one or both can feel tired and maybe have drunk a little too much alcohol. So a night of passion may be unlikely.

So take the pressure off yourselves and remember you have the rest of your lives together. Enjoy being together, just cuddling up. It's just as nice to experience intimacy without having full sex.

The honeymoon

Nowadays, many couples quite wisely delay their honeymoon until sometime after the wedding. Whilst it's nice to get away and relax, with all the excitement of the big day, newlyweds may feel too exhausted to travel immediately afterwards. But if you do decide to go away straight after the wedding, remember to be kind to yourselves and each other. Otherwise you will be starting married life experiencing arguments, and the longed for holiday of your dreams may turn into a nightmare – not a great start to the marriage. But even if you do decide to delay your honeymoon, try and spend some time away just being together.

A NEW ARRIVAL CAN BE A BLESSING AS WELL AS A CURSE

I notice so often that the trend is for couples to have a baby within months of meeting each other, feeling that will cement their relationship. The problem here is that they haven't had time to get to know each other, and allow themselves to settle into the reality of the relationship before introducing another little person into their relationship. Also see Chapter 12 about blended families, where I talk about the additional problems that can arise where children from previous relationships enter the equation.

Once the Romantic stage is over, and the reality of living with each other – the mundanity of everyday life becomes apparent – small niggles can cause arguments that had not arisen before. So adding a small demanding little bundle into the equation can often make matters worse.

Pregnancy is not always the wonderful experience portrayed in the media. Whilst some women sail through pregnancy enjoying every moment, others can be extremely unwell, and ever changing hormone levels can make her moods constantly swing up and down.

Let's also acknowledge the fact that for some women childbirth can feel very frightening and scary. There are always those women who feel duty bound to share their most gruesome stories of childbirth to whoever will listen. Why would you do that to another woman? She needs support and reassurance at such times.

"At this point I will add I had great pregnancies and for me childbirth was amazing. So for any women who have only heard bad stories take note, not every single woman in the world has horror stories!"

Building a strong network of friends and contacts around you is really vital if you don't have that already, as it will support you both once your baby is born. So start building them so that you don't feel isolated as a new mum.

What is often not talked about is that men can often be physically turned off by a pregnant woman, hating their changing shape, feeling uncomfortable about having penetrative sex, worried it will damage the foetus. Other times they perceive the foetus as something alien within their partner. Or they find it hard to cope with the perceived change of their partner from the role of 'Tart in the bedroom' to 'Madonna, and mother of their child'.

All of this can cause stress, arguments, and one withdrawing from the other, causing further upsets. So it's really important you have a strong relationship in which you can share your fears and concerns openly.

Witnessing the birth can also be traumatic and distressing for some men. And all the videos of childbirth cannot prepare for what happens, especially if it involves a long labour, or surgery.

So talking to each other about all of these concerns and worries really will help.

The New Arrival

The baby finally arrives, and hopefully both mum and baby are well, if exhausted.

Following childbirth, a new mother is often sore and perhaps in pain, as well as being totally exhausted, and there is no respite, as it's closely followed by sleepless nights from attending to the never-ending demands of a baby. Babies haven't read the books on being a textbook baby, and don't conform to how they should behave, which can lead the new parents into anxiety, tension and worry about getting it right.

Wherever possible seek and accept outside help, as it will ease the tiredness and stress.

Add to the mix the worries of being new parents, and it's clear that this is not the best scenario for the tenderness and passion that was previously enjoyed.

Dad can feel neglected, as where he was the one his partner focussed all her attention on, he may well feel relegated to second place.

Mum's and dad's focus moves from each other to the baby, often resulting in resentment, as each feels ignored. Arguments become more frequent and the husband can find excuses to work later, go to the pub, or follow other pursuits.

The new mum often hasn't the energy to respond to her partner's sexual requests, and this leads to more feelings of rejection and resentment.

The reason you got together gets lost, and you begin to wonder what you are doing together. This can be one of the flash points, where relationships can break down.

This is where honest communication is so important, if you don't talk to each other and really hear and acknowledge each other, you will often drift apart, making assumptions on what the other is thinking, and why they are behaving the way they are, when the truth can be very different.

> **WHAT FEELINGS COME UP FOR YOU AFTER READING THIS CHAPTER?**
>
> _____
>
> _____
>
> _____
>
> _____
>
> _____
>
> _____

BLENDED FAMILIES

With so many people divorcing or relationships breaking up, there seems to be many more lone parents bringing up children. So quite often when people find new partners, one or the other is likely to have children from a previous relationship. This can add additional strains to the relationship.

- Financially – where maintenance payments are needed to help support the children from the previous relationship.
- Practically – facilitating access between children and biological parents.
- Emotionally – where there is animosity between previous and current partners.
- Children's emotions as they try to deal with the changing circumstances. This can include settling into current families, often with step/half siblings.

Children need access to spend time with the parent they are not permanently living with. Sadly, too often I witness adults using their children as weapons against each other. It can involve withholding maintenance payments, or involving issues around access. Let's remember that access is foremost for the children to be able to have a relationship with their absent parent. The needs and wants of the parent are secondary. The parents are adults who brought the child into the world and are therefore responsible for that child's wellbeing; of course, unless there are sound reasons when access would be detrimental to the child, such as in cases of abuse.

How sad it is when the children are dragged into issues between their parents and a situation they are probably extremely distressed about anyway. Their whole world has been turned upside down, with their family life disintegrating. They don't need to be punished further, unable to spend time with each of the parents they love and miss.

It isn't easy juggling your new relationship as well as the activities of the children that need to be factored in – and let's not forget those special events such as birthdays and Christmas, where each parent understandably wants to spend time with their offspring. If each of the current parents has children from previous relationships, organising all of this can take time away from each other and can cause disagreements and arguments. So again all of this needs some thought, and discussion beforehand, so that resentment doesn't build up.

When a couple then go on to have a child together, the additional responsibilities can make life difficult. As well as juggling time so they have quality time together, there must be time for the existing children, so that one child doesn't feel marginalised, or less important than their sibling.

Parenting styles can be very different from one person to another, and clashes can arise when it comes to acceptable behaviour and discipline. I often see couples who get into real battles because one feels the other is too soft or too hard on the child from a previous relationship.

Many times there are difficulties because the non-biological parent cannot exert authority in the same way as they would if the child were their own.

Children can feel upset and angry – voicing their feelings in the only way they know how. Who has heard that phrase, *"You are not my mum/dad!" "You can't tell me what to do!"* To be on the receiving end of these comments can sting, and adults can lash out.

I think you can see how important it is to communicate

with each other about these situations so as to nip issues in the bud before they become real problems, resolving any that arise. Discuss them on your own, rather than in front of the children, and then you can present a united front. It's also much better to discuss them at the start rather than waiting 'til being in the middle of a maelstrom, and trying to dig yourselves out of it.

> **MAKE A LIST OF ANY ISSUES YOU ARE STRUGGLING WITH**
>
> _____
>
> _____
>
> _____
>
> _____
>
> _____
>
> _____

I NEED TIME ON MY OWN!

When you become a couple and start living together, there are all kinds of things to consider that you didn't have to when you were autonomous and living alone. For example, you didn't have to consider the other person. You could get up and go and do things whenever you wanted to without a thought. And you could choose whether you spent time on your own or with someone else.

Suddenly, you are in a relationship and there is someone else to think about. Initially, you may want to be together all the time. But after a while, as you settle into everyday life, you may become less attentive and thoughtful towards each other. You don't want to spend so much time together, and you start missing your friends or being able to spend time alone. You may either feel claustrophobic or neglected.

This can trigger each other's sensitivities, and can inadvertently cause upset and arguments. One may feel smothered and the other neglected. One person may need more time alone than the other, and/or may want to see other friends. If you don't deal with these situations resentments can build up. With one feeling they cannot see their friends alone.

> **THINGS YOU MAY WANT TO DISCUSS WITH YOUR PARTNER AROUND TIME FOR YOU, WHICH MAY INCLUDE THE FOLLOWING.**
>
> - How much time you need on your own and together
>
> - Which hobbies and pastimes you want to share with your partner
>
> - Which hobbies and pastimes you would prefer to do alone, and how your partner feels about this
>
> - Whether you attend all extended family events together or on your own
>
> - Mealtimes: when you eat and where
>
> - Bedtimes, which can depend on what time you have to get up in the morning, and how much sleep you need
>
> - Other

"We are all human, with human failings."

At the start of a relationship you probably put your partner on a pedestal, but as they revealed more about themselves, you began to feel disappointment that they are not as perfect as you believed them to be.

You may wonder what happened, why has the other

person changed? The thing is the other person probably hasn't changed, although each of you are more likely to be more relaxed around each other, and not on your best behaviour, revealing more of the less appealing sides of yourselves. Because you feel more comfortable with each other, you may not put as much effort into the relationship.

Sometimes clinging to the romantic fantasy, unable to accept the reality of the other person and denying the fact this person you fell madly in love with has warts and failings, can exacerbate your feelings of disappointment.

You start to feel hurt over forgotten occasions, birthdays, anniversaries, things the other says, or a sense of being taken for granted.

Or perhaps you start noticing traits in the other that you really don't like that are totally unacceptable. I talked about core beliefs in Chapter 3 - What makes you and your partner tick?

THE POWER STRUGGLE

Once the Romantic or Honeymoon Stage of a relationship moves into reality, we begin to notice that life is perhaps not as idyllic as you first experienced. You may start feeling your partner is becoming stubborn about issues for no apparent reason, or taking over, wanting things all their own way. Or maybe you feel they always want the last word and the final decision. This leads to arguments over just about everything and anything, and they can be really petty.

"Don't move my things."

"It's your turn to load the dishwasher – I did it last time."

The problem is that when one digs in their heels, the other one is likely to do the same, and you have stalemate, with each of you feeling powerless in the relationship, just not knowing which way to turn. As a result, you may try and exert your power over the other, having that last word – standing your ground. This often results in confusion, trying to appease the situation. But instead of resolving the situation, feelings of being bullied, and ruled by an emotional dictator start to emerge. This can lead to one or the other withdrawing physically and emotionally, becoming cold towards each other.

Alternatively, the inevitable arguments start in retaliation. Sadly, neither of you can recall what the initial argument was about. It all seems quite pointless and draining.

Feelings and thoughts about leaving the relationship arise because you can't stand the rows any more. Or maybe you can't cope with silences from your partner, which you perceive as sulking. They won't talk or discuss what the issues are, or the reason for the silences.

You have had enough, and you wonder where the person you fell in love with has gone!

So before you high-tail it out of the relationship, sit down and talk to each other. Because it's important to discover why your partner is upset or annoyed about things as well as understanding any underlying issues that are going on. Only by talking to each other openly and honestly will you resolve matters.

Start by telling your partner that you value your relationship, and because of that you want to understand.

Using the example of the dishwasher…

- "Our relationship is really important to me, and there seem to be things going on that spark arguments, which is making us both unhappy."
- "I realise that it's important to you that we take turns to load the dishwasher. It's something I'm not bothered about, so I don't understand why you are. Can we talk about it?"
- "What are the other things that are important to you?"
- "Can you help me understand why they are important?"

Whilst the example of the dishwasher may seem trivial, I have only used it as an a starting point. The conversation can be adapted to any situation. The important point is that your partner notices you are interested in them and their feelings. I talk more about this in the next chapter.

> **HOW CAN YOU PHRASE THE CONVERSATION WITH YOUR PARTNER TO ACHIEVE A MORE POSITIVE OUTCOME? WRITE DOWN A FEW IDEAS AND SAY THEM OUT LOUD TO YOURSELF FIRST**
>
> _____
>
> _____
>
> _____
>
> _____
>
> _____
>
> _____

What are the real underlying issues?

These petty arguments are not really about the dishwasher, or your things being moved; there are much deeper emotions going on. The adjustment of being in a relationship, or losing autonomy or sense of self, are more likely to be affected, which is important to each of us, and what we all need.

Whilst it's a wonderful feeling being in a partnership with that special person, someone you care for deeply – maybe the parent of children you adore – you may also feel lost in the relationship.

MY EXPERIENCE

I clearly remember those feelings. It was as if my identity was measured by the fact that I was someone's wife and the mother of my children. I felt I wasn't accepted in my own right, I had lost part of the real me. I loved everything about my wonderful husband and children, as well as being a wife and mum. I just needed something else. I think that was where my marriage started to go wrong, as my husband complained I was doing too much outside of the family. He just didn't seem to understand, and I wasn't able to convey my feelings coherently. We just didn't have the insight or understanding of each other's needs.

So if this happens to you, sit down and talk to each other. You may not really understand what is going on, but by being interested in what each other has to say, unravelling it together, and with a willingness on both parts, you are likely to get to the bottom of it.

Choose your battles wisely

Step back for a moment and ask yourself if the things you are arguing about are really important issues, or minor irritations. Do you find the minor issues are escalating into much bigger rows to the point you don't even remember what the initial issues were? If you recognise this happening, one of you has to stop playing the game or it will become more and more destructive.

Wanting the other to change

It's so easy to want the other person to change, believing it's all their fault, wanting them to change and be the person that suits you. Just think how it would feel if your partner wanted you to change to fit their expectations!

You fell in love and developed a relationship with someone who has their own ways of being in the world, and I am guessing you loved them for the qualities they have. So why do you want them to change into someone else just to fit in with you? Do you really want a clone of yourself? Be prepared to accept them for who they are.

Examples of this might be:

- a lover of the countryside, who enjoys the freedom of being able to spend time outside, and follow outdoor pursuits, being coerced into moving to an apartment in the middle of a town
- a fervent football supporter being nagged for going to football matches
- someone criticising the way their partner dresses

If you are constantly complaining and grumbling at your partner, wanting them to change, you are more likely to build up resentment, as well as hostility, accusations, sarcasm, and sniping. A really unpleasant atmosphere, for sure. You may also drive your partner away.

GOOD NEWS – THERE IS ANOTHER WAY!

If things aren't going well, don't ignore it in the hope it will go away. The issues and niggles are likely to come up again and again, and those resentments will build. It may take many years, but at some point if you don't address the problems, one of you may decide you have had enough and walk away, because so much dissatisfaction and unhappiness has built over time.

I sometimes see couples where one tells me they have been unhappy for a long time, sometimes years, and the other is completely oblivious of this.

Not only is it sad that one person has been so unhappy, but it's very unfair on the other person to receive such shocking news.

The conversation

Sit down and talk to each other in a loving way. Explain to your partner how unhappy you are with the situation, that you feel sure they are as unhappy in the relationship as you are. Without blaming each other, discuss ways in which you feel the relationship isn't working, and then work together to find ways in which you can improve it. Offer ways in which you can help the relationship to work better.

A suitable time and place

Before starting this conversation, choose a time and

place, and don't just launch into it. If you or your partner are distracted by other things, you are certainly not in the best frame of mind to give this your full attention, and it's likely to end up in yet another row.

Don't play the blame game

It's important you don't point the finger at your partner, as that will certainly inflame the problem. If you take the view that it's the relationship that's not working as well as you would both want, it's the relationship that needs working at together. This takes away any blame, and you are both likely to feel less defensive. You then have the opportunity to look forward, in a more positive way.

How to have the conversation

Start by telling your partner that you value them, and that you want things to improve, and then go on to explain how you are feeling, using the "I" statement. By owning your feelings, not only is it powerful, but as I have already said, it's not accusatory, and less likely for your partner to flare up and defend themselves.

Use phrases like –

- I feel really unhappy about some of the things that are happening between us
- I think that something isn't working as well as it could
- I am sad that we keep arguing over such trivial things

Listen to what your partner has to say, without interrupting. Yes, they may rant for a few minutes, but try not to say anything. Let your partner know you are paying attention, and stay fully engaged with them. That means keeping good eye contact, without staring. Use open body language, really look as though you are fully engaged with them.

Instead of trying to defend your corner, and retaliating,

be interested and curious at what they have to say.

I suggest the following formula –
1. Empathise with your partner
2. Own your feelings by using the 'I' statement
3. Listen respectfully, without interrupting
4. Acknowledge your partner's feelings

> **PLAN YOUR TIME, PLACE AND WHAT YOU WANT TO DISCUSS**
>
> - When are the best times for a discussion?
>
> - Where are the best places to have the discussion?
>
> - Pick one issue you want to talk about
>
> You really don't have to agree with your partner, but you do need to acknowledge each other's point of view. Once you have reached a satisfactory conclusion, and the issue is resolved, let it go.

Here is part of Jan and Mike's story that they brought to me.

Jan and Mike had been together for 3 years and they believed their relationship was almost perfect. They congratulated themselves on the fact that they didn't argue like the other couples they knew.

That was until something happened that upset Jan, where she felt Mike had sided with one of his friends rather than her. Jan had stormed off in anger, and left the party they were attending. Mike was annoyed with Jan leaving without telling him where she was going. Huge rows ensued, to the point they could no longer talk to each other about anything, and they both agreed they could not continue in the relationship. It was not only destroying the relationship but themselves too.

They had talked about it, but they really hadn't listened to each other. Before Mike could finish his explanation, Jan was interrupting because she couldn't understand what Mike had said. This was mostly because she was too angry to hear, but also because she didn't agree with the way Mike had behaved. Mike then switched off, and didn't engage with Jan.

By working with them, I encouraged each of them to listen to each other carefully, without interrupting. I asked them to be more curious about what the other's feelings were and try to understand their point of view.

Then the magic started to happen. Jan began to understand why Mike had supported his friend, and actually in that situation he had taken that decision to protect Jan, otherwise the situation could have become very unpleasant. Jan started to understand this, at the same time also understanding why this had pushed her buttons, and the reasons for her uncontrollable anger, which had nothing to do with Mike, but were issues from past relationships. By talking about it in this way, they both had a better understanding about each other.

They didn't need to agree with each other, as that would never be achievable if we accept we are each individuals, with different views. The important part was listening to each other, feeling heard and acknowledged by the other. They both agreed they had not wanted to cause the other distress. Mike didn't want to cause a scene at the party, and Jan left because she didn't want the party disrupted.

The couple acknowledged the relationship still needed to be worked on, especially relating to trust, openness and honesty. Jan finds it difficult to let go of her anger and resentment, still not fully understanding Mike's behaviour. She is relating it to her way of being, how she would behave in the same situation. Jan can't get her head around the fact that Mike has a different way of being and view of the world.

Mike cannot understand what all the fuss is about, and why they can't move on. In this particular area they are out of alignment, and so the work has centred on negotiating between them how far they can meet each other's needs. Because they love each other, the basis of their relationship is strong, and they want to stay together, so they are prepared to work at it.

They have a strong commitment towards each other and to making their relationship work. They are caring towards each other, and show that in many ways. The one part of the three Cs that needs more work is communication, which is what I talked about in Chapter 3.

IS THIS REALLY OK IN A RELATIONSHIP?

Each person has strong feelings about what is intolerable for them. These are the areas which are commonly brought by clients as concerns in their current relationship.
1. Abuse
2. Affairs
3. Addiction
4. Constant arguments and rows
5. Drifting apart
6. Loneliness

Abuse

Abuse is not confined to physical abuse, it also includes sexual or emotional abuse between two people in a close relationship.

It encompasses -
- Physical assault
- Sexual abuse
- Rape
- Threats
- Intimidation
- Degradation
- Mental and verbal abuse
- Humiliation
- Deprivation

- Systematic criticism
- Belittling

This behaviour is damaging not only to those directly involved but also to other members of the family, especially the children. If the cycle doesn't stop, it is likely to continue from generation to generation.

These issues need addressing immediately, or in severe cases, for the partner to end the relationship. This is not always easy and straightforward, so seek advice and support as there are organisations that are specialists in this area.

Affairs

I have written a whole chapter about Affairs in Chapter 17, as I feel it is quite complex.

However, cheating does not automatically mean the end of the relationship, if both partners want to stay together and are prepared to work at the relationship. Affairs are often a symptom that there are other issues going on within the relationship, which need to be addressed.

Addictions

If someone has a drug or alcohol addiction, it is unlikely they will be fully engaged or committed to the relationship. Their relationship is with the drug or alcohol of their choice. They will put the addiction before everything else. Added to this, it's likely to involve lies and deceit, as the dependent person tries to hide the level of dependency to themselves and others. So in these circumstances, if the couple want to stay together, each person who is dependent on their addiction needs to seek help to deal with it. Without taking those steps and being committed to kicking the habit they cannot begin to be committed to the relationship. Kicking the habit is not easy, but it's possible and if you care about your relationship enough you will do it.

Arguments and rows

These are often about trivial matters, but are normally about much deeper issues. Possibly things that haven't been resolved from the past. If they are destroying you and your relationship, making it toxic, it may be better to part company, and end the relationship. But if you want to stay together, and it's just a blip in the relationship, with hard work and honest communication, relationships can be healed and stronger bonds made. See Chapter 15 about how to handle arguments more effectively.

Drifting apart

This is basically where couples neglect the relationship, and there can be many reasons why this happens. With hard work and commitment to work through it, relationships can be saved, and enriched. Communication is the key, as well as focussing on each other. It's far more valuable to consider and work at what you can give to the relationship, rather than feeling resentful about what you are not getting out of it.

Sadly, some couples leave it so long that they have drifted so far apart they cannot and do not want to rebuild bridges.

Loneliness

Some people are worried about leaving a relationship because they are afraid about being alone. Or that no one else will want them. They feel that being in a bad relationship is better than being alone. I don't think this is reason enough to stay, as you can be just as lonely within a relationship.

The effect on us when things go wrong

When things go awry in a relationship, due to constant arguments, or you feel your partner has withdrawn from you, there can be a real sense of rejection and abandonment. In turn, you may withdraw as you feel vulnerable. This can then turn into a stand-off, with each person examining every word and action from the other.

As you become more distant towards each other, you may fear the relationship is ending. You search for endless reassurance, or ask what you have done wrong. Instead of this helping, it often makes matters worse, as you don't get those reassurances. The other person may shut down, or just brush things aside, not wanting to address your concerns.

As a consequence, feelings of lack of self-esteem and self-worth arise. Ask yourself whether the relationship is having a negative effect on your self-esteem and self-worth. Are there things that you and your partner can work on together, that can help improve them and your feelings of loneliness within the relationship?

It's so important to have a strong network of friends and family around you, but at times when you feel isolated, especially when issues within the relationship cannot be resolved, it is more important than ever so you don't feel so lonely. Then if you decide the relationship is not working and the only solution is to leave, you will feel supported and have a network to talk to and be there for you.

Feelings of insecurity

These feelings may be related to earlier issues in your life. Perhaps you were abandoned by a parent, through divorce or death. Or conceivably those strong bonds were not developed with your caregiver. You may have spent time in Children's Homes, with family members or boarding schools. In Chapter 4 I talked about the Attachment theory and how this can affect us in adulthood.

Fear of being abandoned can also be triggered by experiences of former relationships, making you concerned it will happen again. This can then spiral into feelings of not being good enough, that you are not worth anyone better, or believing that all relationships are like this.

At times like this it's worth examining these thoughts and beliefs and checking what evidence you have to support these beliefs. Then list all the things that disprove your theory. You may be pleasantly surprised, or maybe not. But at least you can base your thoughts on evidence rather than fear. Then talk to your partner, because that is the only way you can build a better relationship, and even save it.

AFFAIRS CAN BE COMPLEX

In my experience there are many reasons people have affairs outside their committed relationship.

It can feel quite flattering that someone should notice you, pay a compliment, flirt a little. But there is a difference between that and taking it further and cheating on your partner.

If you have lost that emotional connection with your partner, due to boredom, or feeling dull or dead inside, you may feel you want something more. The grass can certainly look greener on the other side, especially when communication has broken down and the relationship has become neglected.

Before you get swept away with all the wonderful feelings that another person paying attention gives you, STOP and think about what you are putting at risk.

If your partner discovers it, there is likely to be a lot of upset and hurt, even to the point of the breakup of the relationship.

Affairs are not necessarily about sex. They can be about excitement and the longing for something you can't really have. The secrecy of the affair seems to add to this. The fact that the other is unavailable can make it feel safe – or even thrilling. These can add to the feelings of passion and tension that may have been lost in your relationship.

In this day and age, we live in a culture in which we have an expectation and belief that we deserve and have a right to be happy. If we don't feel happy in our relationship, we look outside, believing that we could be happier with someone else, instead of working at the relationship we are currently in. We don't stop and wonder why our current relationship isn't working, we just believe we are with the wrong person, never thinking about the part we are playing, how our behaviour could have an effect on the partnership.

The problem is, if we continue in the same pattern, searching for the happiness that seems to evade us, we are likely to go from one relationship to another, seeking what we perceive as the perfect relationship, in which all our needs are met. This is a totally unrealistic expectation.

There are different reasons for having affairs and I describe each below.

You have been in the relationship for a while and you feel bored

The magic seems to have gone, and you may feel taken for granted. Perhaps you are beginning to feel less attractive. Intimacy has dwindled, maybe sex has become functional, or is not happening at all. Someone new makes you feel alive, sensual. Or possibly your partner no longer seems interested in what you have to say, or spend time with you. Someone else does seem interested and so you find companionship.

Discovering that someone is interested in you, hanging on your every word, and wanting to know more about what you have to say is very attractive.

Loss of Identity

You feel closed in, suffocated, not wanting to spend all your time with your partner because it feels like it's all on their terms. You feel like you have lost your identity, and you just don't know who the real you is anymore. Your confidence has gone, and you are scared your life is closing in on you. You are beginning to feel trapped, not only by the other person, but by the relationship. You want to rebel and act out before life passes you by.

Neglect

You no longer feel you are the most important person in your partner's life. They are either distracted by a new baby, their career, their mates, or their hobbies. You hardly seem to spend any time together. You just don't feel valued, and you wonder what you are doing in this relationship. Someone else paying you attention, turns your head and you start to feel vibrant and live again.

The Exit

You have reached a point of no return. You really don't want to be with this person anymore – you want out, but you don't know how to tell them. By having an affair with someone else, and maybe allowing your partner to find out without having to tell them, you don't have to get involved in arguments or discussions or even be persuaded by your current partner to stay.

The problem here is that you are going to have to face the fallout of this. Your partner is unlikely to accept this situation calmly, unless they feel the same about the relationship. You will still have to live with yourself, that you have cheated, and so often I see couples who keep repeating this pattern in one relationship after another. They never seem to find the happiness they seek.

Three-Legged

A stabilising or three-legged affair often occurs when there is something unfulfilled within the current relationship.

It could be that you feel dissatisfied with sex, or you and your partner just don't talk anymore – you have lost connection and you want companionship.

Some relationships can function and survive this type of three-way relationship. Some even flourish, often in circumstances when one of the partners suffers ill health. Even if your partner is aware of it, and on the surface sanctions it, there may come a time when they feel they have had enough, and are not prepared to continue in this way. Or the other person may decide they don't want to be the third leg and then you each have to face the relationship without the prop.

Revenge

Your partner has done something that has upset you. Perhaps they have had an affair, and you just want to pay them back. You feel if it's good enough for them, then it's good enough for you!

When it's discovered, it leaves each of you feeling upset and hurt, nothing has been resolved by your actions, and the danger is that one affair follows another, as you each try to feel you have the upper hand.

The 7 Year Itch – or Any Year Itch for that matter

You are not getting any younger, and you just want to check you are still attractive to others. Or maybe you feel your partner is past their 'sell by' date. You want to feel you still have what it takes.

If you find that younger person, will you continually be trying to keep them? Concerned they won't want to be with someone older who maybe doesn't have the same interests as they do?

Time to consider when that itch will be satisfied!

Should I stay or should I go?

There is often a sense of guilt from staying in a relationship in which you are unhappy, and a sense of trying to make it work rather than leaving it. Perhaps you are staying for the sake of the children, or because you cannot bear to hurt the other person.

You may have concerns that by taking one action or another, either to stay or leave, you will be judged by your family and friends. That adds to the pressure you feel, not allowing you to make the decision that is right for you.

Before making any decisions about leaving, I think it's

important to explore every avenue.

I would add here that I am not talking about abusive relationships; if this is happening in your relationship then I believe you should leave it. It's toxic and in its worst state can destroy lives.

Can relationships survive an affair?

I believe they can, and have seen this happen. This is especially true where couples accept responsibility for their part, and who see this as an opportunity to rekindle the love and passion that was missing.

However, there are some important things that need to happen for the relationship to begin to heal.

Firstly, the one who cheated needs to accept responsibility for the way they behaved. Not only should they acknowledge the break of trust to their partner and apologise for cheating but they also need to express their guilt and regret for hurting their partner.

Too often I hear the person who cheated wanting to move on and forget about it. They complain that their partner keeps bringing it up. Whereas, the other person feels angry and upset that their partner does this, because they feel their hurt and distress isn't being acknowledged.

It is also important for the person who has been cheated on to build their self-worth and confidence, by doing things that help them feel good about themselves. Because at this precise moment, they feel worthless. They need to surround themselves with people and things that do this, as well as doing things for themselves that make them feel good.

Instead of asking the damaging questions that involved the sordid details of what went on, such as –

- When and where did it happen?
- Were they better than me?
- Describe what they look like

These questions will keep you awake at night and cause more pain.

It is much more productive and useful to ask questions such as —

- What did this give to you that you weren't experiencing in our relationship?
- What did it mean to you?
- How were you able to express yourself in ways that you couldn't in our relationship?
- What did it feel like when you came home afterwards?
- Are you pleased it's over now?

By having open and honest conversations such as those above, it is possible to get your relationship or marriage back on track, building a stronger and loving bond. And hopefully you will find that passion and desire return to your relationship.

WHAT CONSTRUCTIVE QUESTIONS CAN YOU ASK YOUR PARTNER?

_____

_____

_____

_____

_____

_____

MOVING FORWARD AND BUILDING A GREAT RELATIONSHIP

For this to happen there has to be real willingness on both sides, and an acknowledgement that it's not going to be easy. At times it will feel that you are not making any progress, and even that you are going backwards. You are likely to have concerns that nothing will change, and you may fall back into your old patterns again.

It will take patience on both your parts. Don't measure your successes or failures on yesterday, last week, last month. Remind yourselves how long things have been going wrong, and if it's been several years, ask yourself if it's realistic for the problems to be resolved in a few weeks.

Remember to take Baby Steps

Recognise that some of the damaging behaviours were previously out of your awareness, and as such you could not change them. You can't change what you don't know about!

By talking to each other and being more aware you are better able to make changes.

Whilst it's important to talk through the issues that have caused the problems, use them as lessons for the future, rather than keep harping back on the past. This is destructive and doesn't help the situation. It's far more likely to keep you stuck.

You are certainly going to have to make changes to some of your ways of behaving, because –

*"If you always do what you always did, you will always get
what you always got!"*

Begin to see this as an exciting chapter in your relationship. One of self-discovery as well as learning more about each other.

Whilst you may think you know everything about yourself and each other and that it's not worth the effort, you may be pleasantly surprised to learn that there are things you don't know.

I learn something new about myself all the time. I find this exciting and revealing. For instance, I had no idea that I would write a book or get it published. That was until I explored the possibility!

What's possible and what isn't

We each have our own limitations where we are willing to make changes to our lives and our way of being in the world. I believe there may be a ceiling to which we feel we cannot challenge ourselves beyond. But my ceiling is made of glass, because there are things I don't feel comfortable to challenge myself about right now, but beyond the glass I can see things that I could challenge myself about in the future.

We only have to look around us at the role models in the world who have achieved the most amazing feats and refused to accept they have a glass ceiling which cannot be pushed through.

However, that is because that person wants to take up those challenges for themselves alone, and not necessarily because they were someone else's challenges.

Remember to accept and be respectful of the fact that each of you has your own ceiling. How much you can change, and are able to do so, may not be aligned with each other's.

There is really no point of being in a relationship with someone and then spending all your time and effort trying to change the other into the fantasy image you have of the 'perfect' partner or the person you want them to be.

When things are not going well in a relationship, and couples are at a loss to how to repair it, they often point the finger at the other, maintaining they need to change. The problem with this is that you have no control over another person, or their thoughts, actions or words.

The only person we have any control over is ourselves

So to keep putting all the problems in your relationship on the other person is unrealistic and unfair. We each have responsibility for things working – or not, as the case may be.

By taking control and responsibility for your part, and at the same time talking with your partner – negotiating with each other about how each of you can work together to make the changes to the relationship to move forward, and accepting each other's limitations, you have a better chance of building a stronger, more fulfilling and happier relationship.

> **WHAT PART HAVE YOU PLAYED IN NEGLECTING YOUR RELATIONSHIP, AND HOW CAN YOU MAKE CHANGES TO IMPROVE THINGS?**
>
> _____
>
> _____
>
> _____
>
> _____
>
> _____
>
> _____

BRINGING BACK THE PASSION AND INTIMACY IN THE BEDROOM

There can be so many reasons why people stop having sex. Some of them are medical, and as this is not my area of expertise I am not going to talk about them. I suggest in these circumstances that you seek medical advice.

What I am going to talk about are those times when sex and intimacy dwindles, because the relationship is in trouble, or because it is adding to the problems in the relationship.

What exactly is sex?

Some people think sex is only about full penetrative intercourse. However, there are many ways in which we can engage in sex, and sometimes it can be fun, satisfying and more sensual to explore them, rather than the 'Wham Bam, Thank You Ma'am' kind that is mainly about relief and self-gratification. That kind of sexual activity can be very boring after a while. If there is no adventure in it and it becomes routine —perhaps the same position all the time — it's no wonder sex dwindles. If you are not adventurous or run out of ideas, there are plenty of books out there.

The first thing you need to do is be comfortable with your own body. Get to know it, explore it, and learn what feels good and what doesn't. I realise this can feel scary or uncomfortable for some. But if you cannot be comfortable with yourself, then you are less likely to be able to be comfortable with your partner. You need to be able to tell your partner what feels good for you, or what doesn't feel so good. If you are uncomfortable about talking about sex, you are less likely to talk about the problems that get in the way.

Talking about it is the best way forward. I don't mean that barbed giveaway line, or sarcastic comment. I mean sitting down and really talking to each other, not passing comments which can be really hurtful.

Sex means different things to each gender. For men it is a way of connecting and showing their love, and feeling they are loved, whereas women get reassurances from cuddling and closeness. These are generalisations, but we need to accept that women and men are different. So that's why it's important to talk to each other and explore your feelings. Once you have a better understanding how each other experiences the world and your relationship, you can start to build a better sex life.

Part of Clive and Sue's story

Clive and Sue talked to me about the lack of sexual contact in their relationship. Clive told me he felt rejected because Sue recoiled from him, and turned her back on him in bed, saying she was tired. When he tried to cuddle her she brushed him aside complaining it was the wrong time – cooking dinner, watching her favourite TV programme.

Sue felt that Clive only wanted her for sex, and never made any physical contact unless it was to touch her sexually, or if he cuddled her he expected sex at the end of it. She felt objectified.

By encouraging them to talk to each other they began to understand where each other was coming from. Clive explained he found it difficult to verbalise his deep feelings of love for Sue, and that by being sexually intimate he was able to express himself through his body. Once Clive realised how Sue felt about feeling objectified, they began to empathise with each other and worked at bringing sex back into the relationship. So instead of rejecting each other, they were able to talk more openly about their feelings, and help and support each other to feel good about themselves.

> **WHAT DO YOU WANT TO DISCUSS WITH YOUR PARTNER ABOUT YOUR FEELINGS ABOUT YOUR SEX LIFE TOGETHER?**
>
> **I HAVE LISTED SOME PROMPTS BELOW, BUT YOU MAY HAVE OTHERS.**
>
> - Frequency
> - Loss of desire
> - What feels good, and what isn't so good
> - Difficulties around orgasm
> - Sex drive and the different levels you may each have
> - How to manage you sex drive
> - How to initiate more exciting sex

Intimacy is King

When I mention intimacy to couples, some people think I am just talking about sex. But it's so much more than that. It's a deeper connection on so many levels.

It's possible to have sex with a stranger, but you can only have intimacy with someone you are in a deep and meaningful relationship with. If you want a healthy marriage or relationship, I believe you really need to have intimacy.

Intimacy is about really being interested in the other person – their core beliefs, their thoughts, dreams and feelings. It's about being able to talk to each other about any subject, being heard and feeling valued, and your views not being dismissed. This can only be achieved by being open and accepting, in other words, communicating with each other.

THE GREATEST BLOCK – VULNERABILITY!

The scariest part of allowing someone so close to you is about allowing your vulnerabilities to be visible to another person.

When we were young, we were probably very trusting and open to others. But through time and experiences, we discovered that by allowing ourselves to be vulnerable, some people used that honesty and openness against us, and when that trust was broken, it hurt like hell.

So it takes a lot of trust in the other person to show our vulnerabilities. We may have to work on ourselves, and feel comfortable in our own skin before doing so. However, if we can, that relationship will be really intimate, and deeply satisfying.

MY **E**XPERIENCE

For me, that feeling of broken trust first occurred when I shared some of my innermost thoughts and feelings with my mother when I was a young teenager. She encouraged me to share my feelings with her, and then proceeded to throw them back in my face, using them against me.

I continually reeled from the emotional blows directed my way. I felt like I had been through open-heart surgery. This happened time after time, because I really wanted to believe that next time it would be different. It damaged my relationship with my mother irrevocably. I felt I could never trust or confide in her again. Because I was so young and going through adolescence with all the insecurities it brought with it, I didn't have the resources to deal with the situation. I found it hard to trust and allow myself to be vulnerable for quite some time.

Gradually I learned to trust my instincts, and how and when to allow myself to open up and show my vulnerabilities, and this has led me to have some amazingly deep and intimate relationships. Of course it hasn't stopped the heartache when those relationships have ended, but I have developed a more robust sense of self, in which I am better able to deal with it.

PASSION BRINGS GREAT SEX

When relationships are cosy and comfortable they don't encourage great sex, and the danger is that relationships become platonic.

So many times I hear the following comments:
- I'm too tired
- I'm watching my favourite TV programme
- The football is on, can't miss this match
- (S)he is always on his phone/tablet
- He only wants sex, it never stops at a cuddle
- I have so much to do!
- I am just not in the mood

A cosy situation, which is so comfortable you don't feel the need to make an effort, is a far cry from the start of the relationship, where you were uncertain of each other. This created a tension between you, a perfect place for passion too.

You may remember how I talked about the Argentinian Tango in Chapter 2, and how that dance is full of tension and passion. Just watching this dance being performed well evokes all kinds of passion for me.

There is a link at the end of the book to a YouTube clip of the Argentinian Tango being performed. And of course there are many more examples to be found.

Of course passion isn't always as easily evoked as when we are first together. It was almost instantaneous then, without much effort at all.

So you have to be more open to new ideas. Foreplay

plays a huge part in passion. Setting the scene makes all the difference. Here are some ideas, but you will need to think of your own.

- Give each other a massage, whether it's hand, foot, shoulder or body
- Bathe together
- Create a candlelit dinner, with candles and soft music
- Go on a date together – just the two of you

Think up things that you don't normally do to add excitement to the relationship. And remember that sex doesn't have to be full penetrative sex.

Touching and kissing can be very sensual and can aid arousal.

This is a place where the partner who finds it more difficult to verbalise their love can express themselves through their bodies. But before that can happen you need to be able to show your vulnerability, and trust each other. By relaxing and letting go, the most wonderful things can happen.

The power of touch

When you first met each other you progressed through a series of touching stages. Testing the water, but also building that passion and desire – brushing against each other, then maybe tentatively putting an arm around the shoulder, holding hands, a kiss, caressing non-sexual areas of the body, and then building up gradually to genital caresses and intercourse.

The problem is that quite often when couples get into a comfortable relationship, they can easily forget that touch can be very sensual and instead they expect their partner to be instantly ready and aroused. Generally speaking, it takes a woman longer to become aroused than a man, and this needs to be acknowledged. It also means that foreplay is key.

Foreplay

By foreplay I mean initially setting the scene, creating the atmosphere in which you both feel relaxed. A place where you pay full attention to each other. If one of you is constantly distracted by text messages from others for example, or by the football match being shown on the screen where you are having that romantic meal, it's not exactly creating the most convivial setting. By setting the initial scene in a sensitive way, eye contact and hand touching become more meaningful, and can lead onto more intimate foreplay later when you are in private. By taking each step slowly, and giving each other your full attention, passion is likely to be aroused in each other.

Massage is a very powerful aphrodisiac, and the use of oils can enhance the pleasurable feelings, as you move from hands and arms to more erogenous zones and discover what each of you enjoy. How you can give more pleasure to your partner will encourage a sense of closeness, increasing the passion in your own body and that of your partner. This is a time when you can express your love for each other in a physical way, and is especially helpful for those who find it difficult to verbalise their feelings for the other.

It's important to acknowledge that full sex may not always follow, and not to see this as failure on either side. But by spending this time together, being open to trying new things and allowing yourself to be vulnerable, it will bring about a more meaningful, deeper and more intimate relationship.

WHAT CAN YOU DO TO IMPROVE THINGS IN THE BEDROOM?

- Setting the scene

- Foreplay

- Ambience

- Other

THE ONLY WAY IS OUT

Deciding to leave the relationship can be either an easy or difficult decision to make, depending on your reasons for leaving.

But it's likely to bring up a lot of mixed emotions, including relief, as you realise it's the right decision, and you have both been unhappy. At the same time, there will be feelings of sadness for the loss of the relationship and all the hopes and dreams you built around it. People are likely to experience the emotions as those encountered in grief and loss –

- Isolation and denial
- Anger
- Bargaining
- Depression
- Acceptance

Of course it's vital to consider how affected any children in the relationship will be. Their feelings need to be handled carefully and sensitively, especially as they are likely to go through the stages of grief and loss too.

Some considerations before making that decision –

'Do I try to make it work or just leave?'

Relationships have their ups and downs, and hardly ever run smoothly. So let's start with a reality check.

- If you have/had a reasonably good relationship with your parents, are there times when they

drive you mad or you just don't want to be around them?
- Does your best friend get on your nerves at times, because of their quirky or irritating habits?
- Do you enjoy your favourite meal ALL the time? Every single day for example?
- Do you have off days when nothing is going to feel right?

So accept it is very unlikely you are going to get on with your partner at all times in the lifecycle of your relationship.

But there are times when you may need to assess the viability of your relationship, and it maybe there have been too many times when you have stayed for the wrong reasons, hoping that things would work out.

MAKE A LIST OF THE FOLLOWING, WHICH MAY MAKE THINGS CLEARER

- Pros of Staying
- Cons of Staying
- Pros of Staying Versus Leaving
- Cons of Staying Versus Leaving

SURVIVING ON YOUR OWN

A fear of coping alone can feel quite scary, not only fearful of being alone, but also lonely.

There are a lot of practical issues that need to be addressed, but that is not my area of expertise. They are likely to include -

- Living arrangements
- Financial issues
- Custody of children
- Division of property and possessions
- Divorce proceedings

There are links at the bottom of this article where you can gain advice on these issues. Before launching into costly proceedings it's important that you get some advice, whether through the Citizens Advice Bureau, or a free consultation with a Family Law Solicitor, and find out the different options.

My expertise is about bringing your attention to the emotional issues and ways in which you can deal with them.

Feelings of loss and abandonment

Many people only see loss in relation to death, but this is not true. You can also have the same emotions when you lose other things in your lives, including the loss of a relationship; even though it may have been your decision.

Whilst you may feel happy that the relationship has ended, there will also be sadness around all the dreams and aspirations you had planned together for the future. You will also have happy memories of the good times and grieve all of the losses surrounding these. So it's important to be kind to yourself.

Rebuilding your life

It's important at all stages of your life to have a good network of friends and family around you, and if you have that it will prove invaluable at this time. You need people who can offer the different things that you need at different times in your life. Not just a shoulder to cry on, but those who have knowledge and expertise in certain subjects, or who can point you in the right direction. It's also important that you have people around whom you can have fun with, as well as people to chat things through with, and who don't tell you what you should be doing and who don't judge you.

Build a strong network around you

If you withdraw from the world you will feel even more isolated, and lonely. So reconnect with those whose friendships which may have become neglected. Seek out new friendships. It could be about getting involved in your community, schools, community centres, volunteering to do things locally. You will find these networks invaluable in so many ways, as well as helping you feel less lonely.

> ### LIST THOSE PEOPLE YOU HAVE IN YOUR NETWORK AND HOW DO THEY MEET YOUR NEEDS
>
> - Friends
> - Family
> - Professional contacts
> - Practical help

Learn more about yourself

You can use this time to reflect on the past relationship. Whilst you may only feel sadness or anger to begin with, as those feelings diminish it's useful to contemplate the part you played in the relationship. Think about the reasons you chose that person, and the part you played in the breakdown – because we all play a part. This is something that can be hard to acknowledge at times.

My Experience

I was involved in an emotionally abusive relationship for several years and initially I felt quite self-righteous that it was all my partner's fault – that he was controlling and aggressive, which he was. However, at some point I recognised that I had played my part by allowing it to happen. Obviously not intentionally, but because I felt powerless and had no self-worth, I kept letting him back into my life, and allowed the toxic relationship to continue, by constantly trying to appease and placate him, in the hope he would stop his bullying behaviour. Finally, I ended the relationship, which left me feeling worthless and my confidence was rock bottom, Once I began to regain this, I needed time to reflect on the whole relationship. So I spent quite some time exploring the reasons why I entered into that relationship, and why I played the victim, by allowing him to behave that way towards me.

Time to Heal

After the breakdown of a relationship, it is pretty normal for you to feel you are worthless and unlovable, wondering why you have been rejected, or why you feel you didn't measure up.

The immediate response can be one of several actions. Either to feel hatred and distrust of all relationships - and possibly the opposite sex – or you may rush into a new relationship without any thought as to whether that person or relationship is the right one. You may play the field, or have one-night stands or flings that leave you feeling dissatisfied because it doesn't improve self-esteem, quite the opposite, in fact. There is no emotional attachment in them, and you can feel like you are just another conquest.

It's common for confidence, self-worth and trust to be dented by the breakdown, but it doesn't make you a bad or unlovable person. You may also doubt whether you can make a decision, let alone trust your decision.

So just allow yourself time to heal, and don't rush into another relationship when all of these emotions haven't been dealt with.

Learn to love yourself again

Until you learn to rid yourself of all the anger, bitterness and critical thoughts around yourself and the broken relationship, you will find it hard to let go and move forward. Learn to forgive yourself for what you see as your failings, whilst at the same time taking responsibility for your part in it. Until you learn to love yourself, you will not be able to love another.

When we are critical of ourselves, we are also likely to be critical of others, and expect them to live up to our expectations. So if you tell yourself you shouldn't make mistakes, then you are likely to have those feelings about others.

Take up the challenge and see your new life as exciting

Have fun

Go out and have fun, learn to laugh again. Even if there are no others around, you can do things for yourself to make you feel good. They could be things you have stopped yourself from doing in the past in your relationship as you felt you couldn't. But there is nothing stopping you now, is there? Only yourself. It can feel uncomfortable initially to do things on your own. But the more you do it, the easier it becomes.

It is also empowering to know that you are not reliant on someone else. You can have fun on your own. Find new interests, and try new things knowing that you are doing them for you. You don't need anyone's permission. This is the beginning of a new and exciting chapter in your life!

CONCLUSION

As this is my first published book, I am very aware there are areas I haven't covered, which leaves scope for further writing in the future. I don't profess to know all the answers; all I have offered are some of the experiences I have had myself and those my clients have shared, together with ways of tackling issues in ways that have helped clients with whom I have worked.

There are certain sections of our community who have specific problems that relate to their circumstances. In the UK we have a rich and varied community which I fully embrace, but it doesn't mean I can begin to fully understand the problems they experience. For example, the LGBT community (Lesbian, Gay, Bi–sexual, and Transgender community), and those experiencing difficulties with sexual issues or cross-cultural relationships. All of these different areas can raise many issues that deserve specialist support to help them. There are therapists who are better equipped to address and support these specialist areas.

If you have any questions or comments, feel free to contact me.

Thank you for reading this book.

Wendy

CONNECT WITH ME

Facebook - https://www.facebook.com/Copewelltherapies/

Twitter - @CapewellTherapy

Website - www.howtochangemyrelationship.co.uk

Email – relationshipspecialist1@gmail. com

LinkedIn - https://uk.linkedin.com/in/wendycapewell

Skype – wendy1184

If you are reading this as an e-book and would like a pdf copy of the exercises, please email me.

I regularly have tips and news on my website, as well as links to exercises that may help you. Click on this link to sign up to my newsletter.

http://bit.ly/relationshipworksheets

ACKNOWLEDGEMENTS

Writing this book has been an interesting and at times exciting project. One I had not envisaged embarking on until very recently. It came about as a result of me realising that some couples either find it difficult to work with a professional, or find it hard to find the time. There are also times when it would be useful to refer clients to a blog I have written or an exercise they could try for themselves. So the idea of putting all this together in one place developed.

I count myself very lucky that I have met so many wonderful people in my life. As the saying goes, people come into our lives for a reason, a season or a lifetime, something I truly believe. The love, kindness and support I have received and continue to from each and every one is immeasurable.

I think social media is amazing, and it didn't let me down when I was searching for the right person to help me publish this book. I put it out there, and so many people responded, with suggestions, ideas, and help.
My daughters are really supportive, celebrating my successes and spurring me on. I am sure you all recognise how important it is to feel backing from those close to us. So my special thanks to them for giving me non-judgemental support and believing in me.
I would also like to express my thanks to the lovely Paul Moses, from Hans3. He is my right hand man, who not only helps me with e-marketing my business, but encouraged me to write regular blogs for my website. This really got me into the habit of writing, and developing my

own style. and this gave me the courage to write the book. There are those people who have given me further insights into helping couples with their relationship problems, which have been inspirations for this book. This has been in the form of training workshops, books and articles. Special mentions to Linda Beton and Yvonne Johnston for their valuable insights and support over the past few years, and to Mary Clegg for her excellent workshops. I also want to express my thanks to those who have encouraged me to take leaps of faith in my quest to help more people achieve the relationship they want rather than existing in it. There are so many, but special thanks to Catherine Watkin and Cathy Simmons. Lesley Cooley has been an amazing friend during the writing and publication of this book.

Many thanks to those people who have helped me produce this book, including my lovely editor, Sue Miller from TeamAuthorUK, transforming my rough manuscript into a readable book. She has been a tower of strength, and I really appreciate her patience during this adventure, guiding me through the process of self-publishing. Thank you too to Ellen Parzer for helping with the design of the book cover.

Finally I want to thank my lovely clients, who have trusted me enough to share their stories with me, and allowing me into the most intimate and precious parts of the lives. I feel so privileged to be allowed to help and support them through the difficult times in their relationships, helping them to reconnect with each other. They have taught me so much and continue to do so.

ABOUT THE AUTHOR

Wendy currently lives in Hampshire, on the borders of Surrey and West Sussex, where she has a thriving business, which is her passion.

In her leisure time she enjoys spending time with her family, who live nearby. She draws and paints – a pastime she took up only a few years ago – and loves to travel whenever she has the opportunity.

Her life has been peppered with a great deal of happiness as well as some really difficult times too. Twice married, each relationship brought both happy and sad times.

She is a proud survivor of breast cancer, with which she was diagnosed over 25 years ago.

This book is Wendy's first, although she writes regular articles for her website and other publications.

TESTIMONIALS

Jane and Peter

This couple came to me after Peter had been drawn to someone outside of their relationship, and understandably Jane felt betrayed. We explored the reasons this had happened, and working together we got to the root of the problem. Before working with me they said,
"There was bad communication between us, and we lacked understanding of each other. This culminated in the breakdown of the relationship."
They had some reservations before working with me, 'wondering how the process would work', however, at the end they said,
"We feel able to talk to each other and verbalise our feelings better."

Gary and Emily

This couple felt that there was little that could be achieved from working with me, and felt their relationship was close to ending.
"Before starting working with Wendy, there was no proper communication in our relationship, which was almost over. We were nervous about seeing Wendy, having seen professionals in the past, that had no effect. I was probably not expecting much. During the process, pretty much something new was unravelled, discovered and explored, which made it an enlightening journey. As a result, we gained a greater understanding of ourselves and each other, recognising flaws, and talking to each other, instead of arguing."

Peter and Grace

This couple were quite anxious about working with me, however once they realised I was not going to take sides or blame either of them, we made some great progress.

"Despite initial reservations about working with Wendy, as neither of us had any experience of working with a professional before, we found the whole process very helpful, and it enabled us both to look at and consider issues and each other's view points in a way that we hadn't been able to do before. Overall, we found it to be a very positive experience."

Amy and James

Amy and James were still adjusting to each other and their relationship. They had experienced many changes in a short space of time, and were struggling with those changes. They were desperate to make their relationship work better, as you can see from what they said below.

"I would like to thank you for assisting my husband and I to resolve some very difficult issues we experienced in the early years of our marriage that we were struggling to overcome on our own. It really helped us to talk to each other again in a controlled and civil fashion, and not get cross with each other.

We are especially thankful to you for going the extra mile to fit in around our childcare issues. We have been able to go from strength to strength and love and respect each other once again. I feel certain the help you provided us will stand us in very good stead for many more years of a happy marriage."

RESOURCES & FURTHER READING

Organisations offering support and help:

Citizens Advice Bureau:
https://www.citizensadvice.org.uk/
Nationals Centre for Domestic Violence:
http://www.ncdv.org.uk/
DV Men: http://www.dvmen.co.uk/
Survivors Trust – Supporting Survivors of Rape and Sexual Abuse:
http://thesurvivorstrust.org/national-helplines/
Women's Aid: https://www.womensaid.org.uk/
Family Law Resolution: http://www.resolution.org.uk/
Alcoholics Anonymous: http://www.alcoholics-anonymous.org.uk/
Drugs Helpline:
http://www.urban75.com/Drugs/helpline.html
An Intimacy App for Busy Couples to Feel Close
http://pillow.io/

Useful Publications

The Grief Book – Debbie Moore
Attachment: Volume One of the Attachment and Loss Trilogy:
Attachment Vol 1 (Attachment & Loss)
Loss (Attachment and Loss) Volume 3 - Dr E J M Bowlby
Mating in Captivity – Esther Perel
Intimacy & Desire – Dr David Schnarch
Stop Arguing, Start Talking: The 10 Point Plan for Couples in Conflict - Relate

Video of Antonia Banderas dancing the Argentinian Tango
https://www.youtube.com/watch?v=6lAKlYTQVKY

Made in the USA
Charleston, SC
06 December 2016